Tools & Trades

The Tools & Trades History Society
Reg. Charity No. 290474

was founded in 1983 to further the knowledge and understanding of hand tools and the people and trades who used them.

The Society publishes a quarterly newsletter and an occasional Journal which the members receive as part of their membership benefits.

The Tools & Trades History Society web site: www.taths.org.uk

All rights reserved. No part of this book may be reproduced, stored in a retrieval system, or transmitted in any form or by any means, electronic, mechanical, photocopying, recording, or otherwise, without prior written permission of the Tool & Trades History Society, except where permitted by law.

Responsibility for all statements, opinions and material contained in the articles printed herein rest solely with authors.

ISBN 0 947673 16 4

© The Tool & Trades History Society 2005

Edited by Jane Rees
Printed by The Joshua Horgan Print Partnership, Oxford

Contents

Abstracts

Articles

The Mark Rees Memorial Lecture 2004
Seventeenth- and eighteenth-century woodworking tools: 1
The evolution of a British style
James M. Gaynor

Science friction, machines, and corrugated planes   30
Warren Hewertson

Scythe makers and other metal workers   46
in the parish of Norton, 1533 - 1750
Kathleen M. Battye

Folk craftsmanship in fruitwood: 78
A seventeenth-century jointing plane dated 1682
Jonathan Green-Plumb

Book Reviews

Luigi Nessi Antique Tools and Instruments   83
Elton W. Hall

Don & Anne Wing Early Planemakers of London: 85
Recent discoveries in the Tallow Chandlers and the Joiners Companies
David Millett

The cover picture:

The picture on the cover is taken from *Fantastic Costumes of Trades and Proffessions, an Album of 36 17th Cent. Engravings* by Gerard Valck (1652-1726) and Nicolas de l'Armessin (1640-1725). Republished in 1969 by the Holland Press Ltd. London.

The plate used is No. 11, the *Habit de Coústellier*, the Clothing of the Cutler.

Abstracts

The 2004 Mark Rees Memorial Lecture
Seventeenth- and eighteenth-century woodworking tools: The evolution of a British style

James M. Gaynor

The evolution of English joinery and cabinet-making tools during the seventeenth and eighteenth centuries is discussed, focusing on chisels and gouges, saws, planes and bitstocks. During those two hundred years, there is convincing evidence of two periods during which tool types and designs underwent surges of change. The first was during the second half of the seventeenth century to the early years of the eighteenth. Based upon archaeological evidence and a few surviving tools, the tools used in England and English colonial America before this period were of a style that was not particularly English, but rather of a more generic western, or northwestern European origin.

By the end of this period, national English tool styles had emerged that were distinctly different from those to be found elsewhere in Europe. The second surge of tool development occurred during the second half of the eighteenth century, most notably during the period from about 1750 to 1780. By the end of this period, English tools had largely assumed their "modern" appearance.

Science friction, machines, and corrugated planes.

Warren Hewertson.

Corrugated bottom planes were sold by many of the makers of metal planes, the marketing implying that they were easier to use than a metal plane with a flat sole due to reduced friction. The author explores this idea, explaining the historical background to the discovery of friction and the scientific causes and effects.

The efficacy of the many designs and patents for a variety of planes with grooved bottoms is looked at in depth and the history of the corrugated bottom plane set out with illustrations of examples from both America and Britain.

Scythe makers and other metal workers in the parish of Norton, 1533 – 1750

Kathleen M. Battye

In a sample of 298 wills and inventories made between 1533 and 1750 by people living in the north Derbyshire parish of Norton, 61 were metal workers, and of these 29 were scythe makers. Transcription and analysis by a class under the tutorship of the author give a full picture of this group of metal workers, detailing the sites they operated, their equipment, raw materials, tools and stock, and their financial position at death. Many had a dual occupation in agriculture and scythe making.

Folk craftsmanship in fruitwood: A seventeenth-century jointer plane dated 1682

Jonathan Green-Plumb

A seventeenth-century jointer plane is studied in relation to its time and place of making and its relationship to other planes of similar date. Alterations to the plane are discussed and theories about the reasons for its preservation are presented.

2004 Mark Rees Memorial Lecture

Seventeenth- and eighteenth-century woodworking tools: The evolution of a British style

James M. Gaynor

There is convincing evidence that there were two periods in which English joinery and cabinetmaking tool types and designs underwent surges of change during the seventeenth and eighteenth centuries. The first occurred during the second half of the seventeenth century to the early years of the eighteenth, about 1650 to 1710 or 1720. The second was during the second half of the eighteenth century, most notably during the period from about 1750 to 1780. That changes occurred is apparent. The factors that stimulated them are much more difficult to identify and substantiate.

The first permanent English settlement in North America was in Virginia. Colonists landed there in 1607, and built an initial fortification along the James River at Jamestown. In the years that followed, the English expanded the area of settlement, principally along the rivers and bays that define the coastal landscape (Fig. 1). For the past fifty years, archaeologists have investigated these early settlements or "plantations". They have recovered a large number of artifacts dating to the seventeenth century, and scattered among them are tools, almost all for woodworking: axes, chisels, augers, drill bits, hammers, and saws.

In the late 1980s, when serious research in preparation for the exhibition *"TOOLS: Working Wood in 18th-Century America"*[1] at Colonial

Fig. 1. Herman Moll's A New & Correct Map of the Whole World, *1719. Eastern Virginia and the Chesapeake Bay area are highlighted. All illustrations are courtesy of Colonial Williamsburg Foundation (CW) unless otherwise noted. Photography by Hans Lorenz and Craig McDougal. CW 1979-289.*

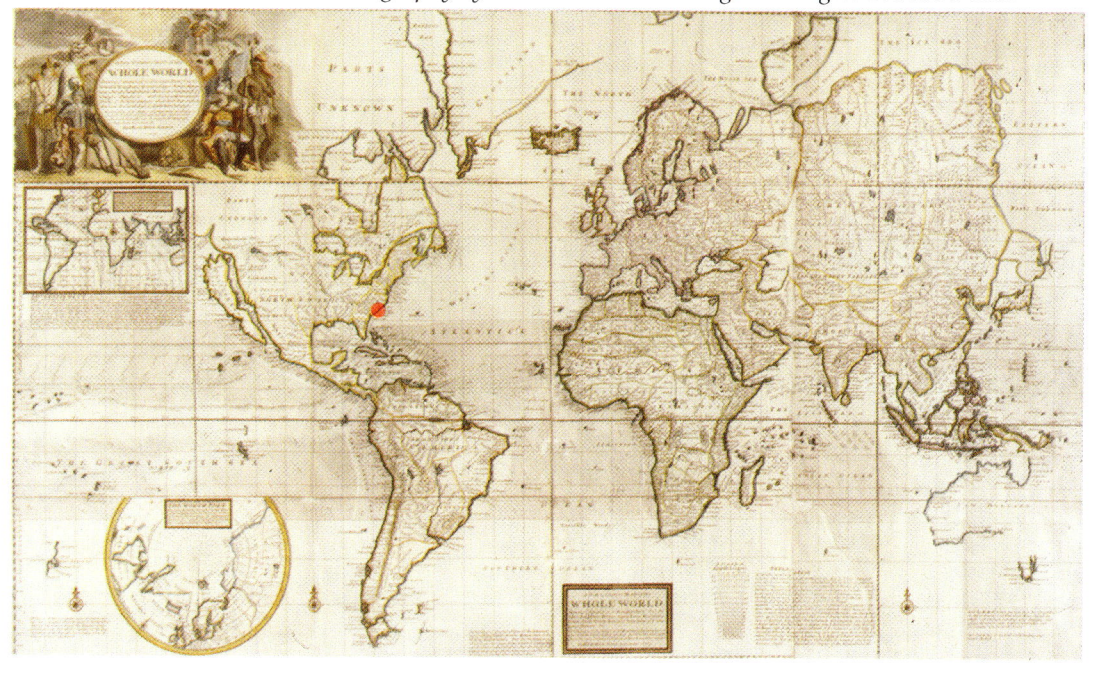

Williamsburg began, it became apparent that studying these early tools was important. A team of researchers spent time at a number of repositories that held the pieces, took photographs, made drawings, and tried to make sense of the group as a whole as well as the individual tools.

For the most part, they were general-purpose woodworking tools, the implements that individual plantation owners needed to clear the land, do some basic building, construct fences, repair agricultural implements, and split firewood (Fig. 2). These are just the types of tools that the Virginia Company suggested its settlers equip themselves with in a broadside published in 1622 (Fig.3). More specialized tools rarely appear in seventeenth-century archaeological sites, or even in seventeenth-century Virginia-area documents. The establishment of specialised trades was a slow process in the colony.

While the *types* of tools for the most part supported what we suspected, the actual forms of the tools were quite a different story. They were not simply "early" versions of what we thought of as typical eighteenth-century English tools. There were drill bits with flat, rather than square tangs; mortise and paring chisels with bolsters that went only three-quarters of the way around the tool; socket chisels that had

Fig. 2. European woodworking tools recovered from seventeenth-century Virginia arch- aeological sites. Top: gouge, axe, and compasses from Martin's Hundred near Williamsburg, ca. 1620-1640. The axe head is 6 5/8" long. Bottom: mortise chisel, tongue-plane iron, saw wrest, drill bit, wedge, and hammer head from Flowerdew Hundred, a plantation on the James River about twenty-five miles west of Jamestown, 1618-1730. Martin's Hundred objects courtesy of Colonial Williams- burg; 7787- 50HA; 7875-50BA; 7788-50HA. Flowerdew objects courtesy of Flowerdew Hundred Foundation. PG3/25; 44PG65/193L1-6; 44PG66/508B1-92; 44PG65/190/53-22; 44PG65/193N3D-4; 44PG64/2C/SWQ.

THE INCONVENIENCIES

THAT HAVE HAPPENED TO SOME PERSONS WHICH HAVE TRANSPORTED THEMSELVES

from *England* to *Virginia*, without prouisions necessary to sustaine themselues, hath greatly hindred the Progresse of that noble Plantation: For preuention of the like disorders heereafter, that no man suffer, either through ignorance or misinformation; it is thought requisite to publish this short declaration: wherein is contained a particular of such necessaries, as either priuate families or single persons shall haue cause to furnish themselues with, for their better support at their first landing in Virginia: whereby also greater numbers may receiue in part, directions how to prouide themselues.

Apparrell.

Apparrell for one man, and so after the rate for more.

	li.	s.	d.
One Monmouth Cap	—	01	10
Three falling bands	—	01	03
Three shirts	—	07	06
One waste-coate	—	02	02
One suite of Canuase	—	07	06
One suite of Frize	—	10	00
One suite of Cloth	—	15	00
Three paire of Irish stockins	—	04	—
Foure paire of shooes	—	08	08
One paire of garters	—	00	10
One doozen of points	—	00	03
One paire of Canuase sheets	—	08	00
Seuen ells of Canuase, to make a bed and boulster, to be filled in Virginia 8.s. One Rug for a bed 8.s. which with the bed seruing for two men, halfe is	—	08	00
Fiue ells coorse Canuase, to make a bed at Sea for two men, to be filled with straw, iiij.s. One coorse Rug at Sea for two men, will cost vj.s. is for one	—	05	00
	04	00	00

Victuall.

For a whole yeere for one man, and so for more after the rate.

	li.	s.	d.
Eight bushels of Meale	02	00	00
Two bushels of pease at 3.s.	—	06	00
Two bushels of Oatemeale 4.s. 6.d.	—	09	00
One gallon of Aquauitæ	—	02	06
One gallon of Oyle	—	03	06
Two gallons of Vineger 1.s.	—	02	00
	03	03	00

Armes.

For one man, but if halfe of your men haue armour it is sufficient so that all haue Peeces and swords.

	li.	s.	d.
One Armour compleat, light	—	17	00
One long Peece, fiue foot or fiue and a halfe, neere Musket bore	01	02	—
One sword	—	05	—
One belt	—	01	—
One bandaleere	—	01	06
Twenty pound of powder	—	18	00
Sixty pound of shot or lead, Pistoll and Goose shot	—	05	00
	03	09	06

Tooles.

For a family of 6. persons and so after the rate for more.

	li.	s.	d.
Fiue broad howes at 2.s. a piece	—	10	—
Fiue narrow howes at 16.d. a piece	—	06	08
Two broad Axes at 3.s. 8.d. a piece	—	07	04
Fiue felling Axes at 18.d. a piece	—	07	06
Two steele hand sawes at 16.d. a piece	—	02	08
Two two-hand sawes at 5.s. a piece	—	10	—
One whip-saw, set and filed with box, file, and wrest	—	10	—
Two hammers 12.d. a piece	—	02	00
Three shouels 18.d. a piece	—	04	06
Two spades at 18.d. a piece	—	03	—
Two augers 6.d. a piece	—	01	00
Six chissels 6.d. a piece	—	03	00
Two percers stocked 4.d. a piece	—	00	08
Three gimlets 2.d. a piece	—	00	06
Two hatchets 21.d. a piece	—	03	06
Two froues to cleaue pale 18.d.	—	03	00
Two hand-bills 20. a piece	—	03	04
One grindlestone 4.s.	—	04	00
Nailes of all sorts to the value of	02	00	—
Two Pickaxes	—	03	—
	06	02	08

Houshold Implements.

For a family of 6. persons, and so for more or lesse after the rate.

	li.	s.	d.
One Iron Pot	—	—	—
One kettle	—	07	—
One large frying-pan	—	06	—
One gridiron	—	02	06
Two skillets	—	01	06
One spit	—	05	—
Platters, dishes, spoones of wood	—	02	—
	—	04	—
	01	08	00

For Suger, Spice, and fruit, and at Sea for 6 men. — 00 | 12 | 06

So the full charge of Apparrell, Victuall, Armes, Tooles, and houshold stuffe, and after this rate for each person, will amount vnto about the summe of — 12 | 10 | —

The passage of each man is — 06 | 00 | —

The fraight of these prouisions for a man, will bee about halfe a Tun, which is — 01 | 10 | 00

So the whole charge will amount to about — 20 | 00 | 00

Nets, hookes, lines, and a tent must be added, if the number of people be greater, as also some kine.

And this is the vsuall proportion that the Virginia Company doe bestow vpon their Tenants which they send.

Whosoeuer transports himselfe or any other at his owne charge vnto *Virginia*, shall for each person so transported before Midsummer 1625. haue to him and his heires for euer fifty Acres of Land vpon a first, and fifty Acres vpon a second diuision.

Imprinted at London by FELIX KYNGSTON. 1622.

Fig. 3. Broadside issued by the Virginia Company in 1622 recommending that settlers equip themselves with a basic kit of woodworking tools. Courtesy of the John Carter Brown Library at Brown University.

Fig. 4. Small joiner's riveting hammer head excavated at Flowerdew Hundred Plantation from a ca. 1690-1730 context. OL: 4". Courtesy of the Flowerdew Hundred Foundation. 44PG66/508A1-53.

six-sided sockets; carving tools that looked more medieval than modern; hammer heads that looked Continental (Fig. 4); and panel saws that seemed akin to traditional Dutch handsaws.

The first explanation was that many of these tools were not English at all. They could just as likely be Dutch, or from other Continental suppliers. Dutch merchants traded considerable quantities of all kinds of Continental goods with the early Virginians. This seemed a satisfactory enough explanation until I had a chance to see some of the tools coming from sites of roughly the same date in England, some found on the Thames foreshore, and a few tools surviving in English museum and private collections. Much to my surprise, the same tool

Fig. 5. Mortise chisel with three-quarter bolster excavated at Flowerdew Hundred from an undated context. OL: 7 ¼". Courtesy of the Flowerdew Hundred Foundation. PG3/25.

forms showed up: similar saws, hammers, and chisels.

The mortise chisel shown in Figure 5 with a ¾-bolster is from Flowerdew Hundred Plantation and most likely dates to before 1650. The top and bottom edges of the blade are parallel,

Fig. 6. Paring chisel from a 1680-1710 context at Causey's Care, a site in Charles City County, Virginia, about 30 miles west of Jamestown. OL: 10". Courtesy of the Virginia Department of Historic Resources. CC178/50A.

or possibly have a bit of the reverse taper of mid-eighteenth-century English mortise chisels, taller at the edge than at the tang. Other than the bolster, the chisel is not dissimilar to later mortise chisels. The same is not true for paring chisels. They tend to be almost spatula-shaped, tapering to a very thin front edge (Fig. 6). Shanks are long. Blades are essentially parallel. Some, like one from the collections of the Science Museum in London, have bevelled sides (Fig. 7).

Fig. 7. Paring chisel. OL: 12 3/8". Courtesy of the Science Museum/Science & Society Picture Library. 1951-226.

Another, also from the Science Museum collection, shares these details, as well as filed decoration on the upper corners of the blade. In addition it has a decorated shank, and is stamped with the name "CARL(E?)

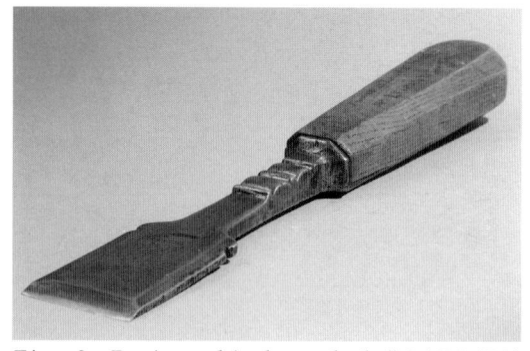

Fig. 8. Paring chisel marked "CARL(E?) MOOR(E?)" in two zigzag-border intaglio marks. OL: 12 1/8". Courtesy of Science Museum/Science & Society Picture Librbary. 1951-227.

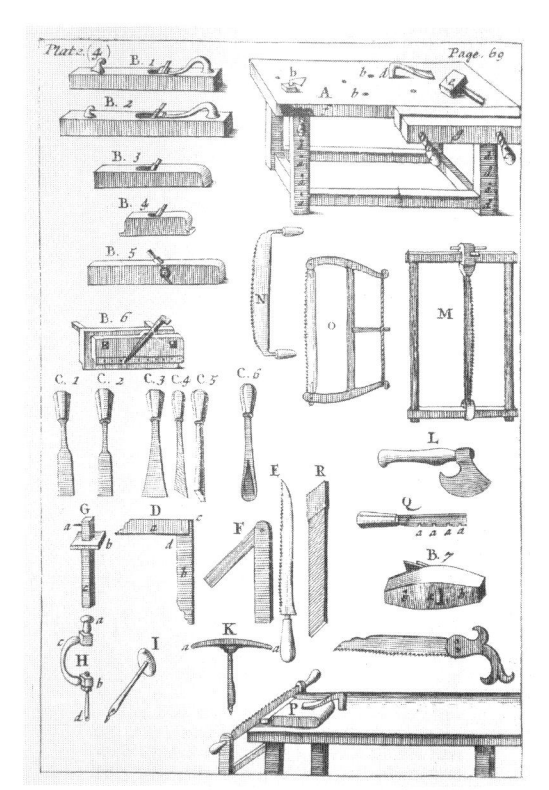

Fig. 9. Tools of the joiner. Plate 4 from Joseph Moxon's Mechanick Exercises, or the Doctrine of Handy-Works *(London, 1703 edition).*

MOOR(E?)" using two separate stamps (Fig. 8). The few gouges recovered have long, tapering blades. These tanged chisels and gouges bear a striking resemblance to those illustrated by Joseph Moxon in his plate of joiners' tools

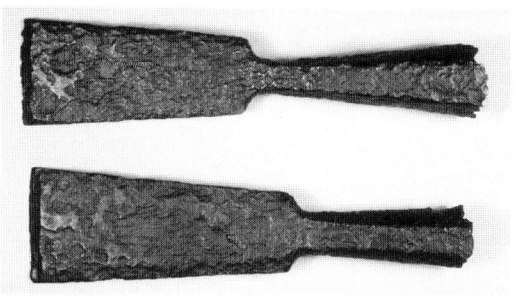

Fig. 10. Hexagonal socket chisels excavated at Yorktown, Virginia. The top chisel is 8 1/2" OL with a 2" blade. Courtesy of the National Park Service Colonial National Historical Park, Yorktown Collection. COLO Y-1610 and COLO Y 952.

Fig. 11. Hexagonal socket chisel marked "SAMUEL FREETH". OL: 13 1/8". CW 9078-O.C.

in *Mechanick Exercises* published initially in 1678 (Fig. 9).[2]

The excavated socket chisels have six-sided sockets (Fig. 10). While narrow ones have parallel, or nearly so, blades, wider chisels flare and typically have narrow bevels on their edges. The chisel in Figure 11 is an especially intact archaeological specimen that dates to the late seventeenth or early eighteenth century. It is marked "SAMUEL FREETH", another surname, like that of "Moor(e)" on the paring chisel in Figure 8, that appears among the documented eighteenth-century edge tool makers of Birmingham. Once more, these socket chisels bear a striking resemblance to

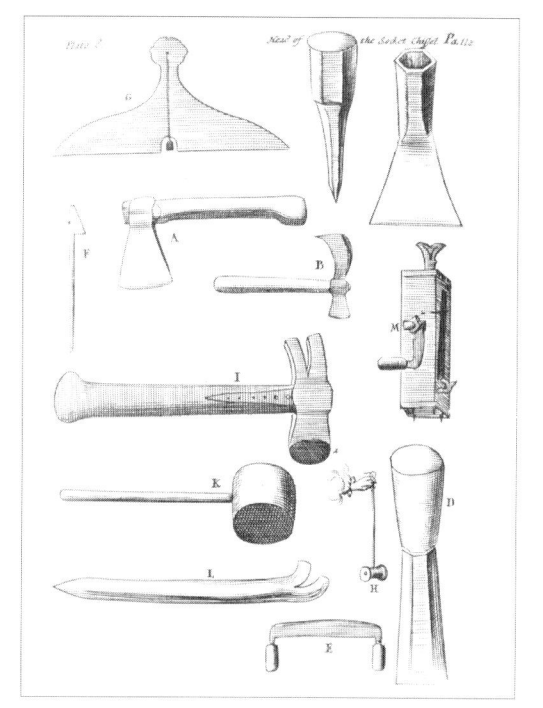

Fig. 12. Tools of the house carpenter. Plate 8 from Joseph Moxon's Mechanick Exercises. *The hexagonal socket chisel is shown at the upper right, with the handle (left) removed from the socket.*

the one illustrated by Moxon, in this case, in his plate of carpentry tools (Fig. 12).

As an aside, these six-sided sockets are a rather difficult form to make. Their only apparent advantage, besides the aesthetic, is that they allowed the user to "feel" where the top and bottom of the blade was when he grasped the tool. It no doubt made tool alignment easier. It may also have resulted in a more secure handle-to-socket fit.

I do not know of any surviving early seventeenth-century handsaws from an English context, leaving us only with the excavated examples. A fragment from Jamestown suggests that it might be the remains of a saw not too different from later Dutch ones, but a virtually entire surviving blade from a Virginia site dating to about 1620 to 1635 has differences in

Fig. 13. Handsaw blade, with toe to the right, excavated at Jordan's Point, near Hopewell, Virginia, in a ca. 1620-1635 context. OL: 25". Courtesy of the Virginia Department of Historic Resources. 44PG302/F-110 EU#766.

detail of the blade shape (Fig. 13). Even more important, the tang for mounting the handle is merely an extension of the blade and emerges from the middle of the saw's heel rather than at its top like most Dutch panel saws. It also appears to have holes for securing the handle with rivets or screws. Again, it looks quite like the handsaw illustrated in Moxon (Fig. 9).

There are not many surviving planes that can be documented to the first three-quarters of the seventeenth century, and the archaeological evidence consists mainly of fragments of bench plane irons (Fig. 14). The tongue plane iron excavated from a circa 1618-1660 context at Flowerdew Hundred and shown in Figure 2 is a rarity, at least on the western side of the Atlantic.

Based on its design, the hollow plane shown in Figure 15 may have been made before 1670. Its length, its visual weight, and the bold architectural nature of its very broad chamfers suggest an early date. The wedge, while a recent replacement, is based upon the original one that survives with most of its upper finial missing. The ogee shaping is present on the original. Interestingly, the shoulder moulding is "stopped" in the same way that architectural mouldings, like chair rails, are terminated: the profile of the moulding is cut at the end of the moulding straight back to the wall, or in this case, to the plane stock. This plane does not look much like the planes illustrated in either Moxon or Randle Holme's *Academy of Armory*.[3]

Fig. 14. Bench plane irons excavated at Jamestown, Virginia. Courtesy of the National Park Service Colonial National Historical Park, Jamestown Collection. COLO J 5823 Ltb23, COLO J 1747 LTB97 F2 STR17, and COLO J 10339 PR194 99:105 SO60.

Fig. 15. Early English hollow plane, beech, maker unknown. The reproduction wedge is based upon the broken original. OL: 10 11/16".Private collection

But there is one document in which all these tools are shown. The Stent panel is familiar to many tool collectors, but it deserves to be studied in detail (Fig. 16). On the wall of the workshop it depicts are planes similar to the one just described. The chisel shapes are similar to those from 17th-century Anglo-American contexts, and the handsaw has a blade shape and handle attachment that are very much like those of the blade recovered in Virginia.

No one knows whether this panel is Dutch or English. Curatorial associates who know ceramics and costume come down on the side of Dutch. Nevertheless, based upon the tools just examined, it accurately illustrates the forms of tools being used in England.

Whether these tools were made in England or imported from the Continent is unknown. Given the extensive trade with the Dutch, especially through the port of Antwerp, where manufactured goods from all over Western Europe could be had, it is likely that many of them are Continental. Regardless, the designs of the tools found on American and English sites suggest that the tools used by both English woodworkers and their colonist brothers were of a style that was not particularly "English," but rather of a more generic western, or north-western European origin.

This brings us back to Mr. Moxon. For a long while he has been accused of borrowing the illustrations for his plate of joiners' tools from the French author André Félibien, who, in 1676, published a book entitled *Des Principes de l'Architecture*.[4] These critics contend that Moxon copied these plates either because he was uninformed about English tools or because it was less trouble to copy existing illustrations than come up with new ones. I have a hunch that neither is the case. Time after time, Moxon mentions details in his text that show he was intimately familiar with woodworking tools. I think it is quite possible that he felt legitimate in copying Felibien's illustrations because they showed what at least many joiners' tools used in England looked like. Dutch, German, and French tools (and maybe some Scandinavian ones as well) probably were widely used in England, especially around the major importing centre of London where Moxon worked, observed, and wrote. It also is quite possible that many tools made in England – again more likely in London than provincial, inland centres – were made to resemble this generic western European style. In several cases where English tools did not conform to the generic styles, Moxon points it out either in his text or in his illustrations, like those of the handsaw, the smoothing plane, and the hexagonal socket chisel. I just wish he had a spent a bit more time making certain his text and illustration references matched up.

Leaping ahead fifty or sixty years, there is ample evidence that English woodworking tools had changed. One of the earliest, if not the earliest, English genre paintings to show woodworkers in action is William Hogarth's *The Carpenter's Yard*, painted about 1727 (Fig. 17). Only a few processes and tools are shown, but, from what can be seen of the handsaw, it looks very much like what we think an English handsaw should look like. The same is true for the pitsaw, of the whipsaw type. Note that, even this early, these carpenters have their badge of occupation: folding rules stuck in their breeches pockets.

Fig. 16. The Stent panel. 14 3/16" by 28 1/8" including frame. Courtesy of Duncan McNab.

Fig. 17. The Carpenter's Yard by William Hogarth, ca. 1727, oil on canvas. Courtesy of Peregrine G. Sabin.

Turning to more precise pictorial evidence from this period, the new tool forms are better defined. The trade card advertising the business of planemaker and tool merchant John Jennion, printed about 1740, shows a tanged chisel of a different, sweeping form (Fig. 18). The handsaw has acquired a new, closed handle and is longer and wider than its seventeenth-century predecessors. The bench planes look English now rather than Continental, and, although the card shows only the sole of a moulding plane, we know from surviving planes made by Jennion that they also are distinctively English. Of the tools we are focussing on, only the bitstock does not look too different from the earliest, fifteenth-century representations. Other sources, like the William Emmett trade card of circa 1731 and the 1747 Mark Sharpe gravestone at Lewes, Sussex, confirm these changes.[5,6]

What led to these transformations during the late seventeenth and early eighteenth centuries? Starting about 1650, and due to war

Fig. 18. Trade card of London planemaker John Jennion, ca. 1740. Heal Collection. Courtesy of the Trustees of the British Museum. 118.8.

and changes in English trading policy, the supply of Continental tools was, if not cut off, at least severely hampered. About the same time, several events and circumstances added to an increasing overall demand for tools in England and her colonies: The Great Fire of London in 1666 and the need to rebuild the city; expanding colonial markets; a generally increasing affluence and the resulting greater demand for goods, whether they be necessities, niceties, or luxuries. Especially in the latter category, English consumers developed preferences for new, more complex, and, from an international perspective, more fashionable household and personal furnishings. Joinery, particularly in the finishing details, became more complex. The trade of cabinetmaking emerged.

In addition to growing demand, other factors – an expanding English merchant fleet; mercantilist economic policies; the availability of capital; and no doubt a host of other converging forces – encouraged English domestic manufacturing in general. Little is known about English toolmaking before this period, but we know that an infrastructure was in place to support its growth. Iron and steel making were developing in size and sophistication. Other toolmaking materials were available domestically. There were toolmakers scattered over the country, and even this early, there were emerging centers of tool production that possessed specialised resources, including pools of skilled labor and advantages ranging from proximity to necessary materials, to water power, to good access to water-born transportation.

Up to this point, "country," i.e., provincial, toolmakers probably made their wares according to local tool styles and sold most of their production either locally or through fairs or chapmen. The curtailing of imported tools may have had little effect on these local, provincial markets, but it must have had an impact on the demand for tools in locations that had been more dependent upon imported goods. The impact likely was felt in London and other trading ports; it may have been greatest for overseas markets that suddenly found themselves largely dependent upon only English goods.

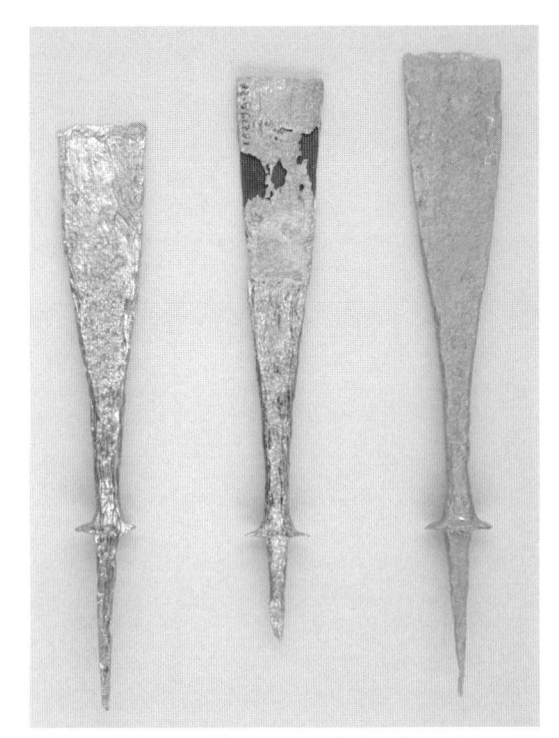

Fig. 19. Several of a group of chisels and gouges excavated at the Anthony Hay Cabinet Shop in Williamsburg, Virginia, from a 1740-1760 context. The chisel on the right is 7½" OL. CW ER206-28D, ER229A-28D, 0071-28D-C.

As a result of increased demand and its changing nature, individual toolmakers expanded. More and more highly specialized toolmakers emerged. Tool merchants began to oversee the production of more individual shops and distribute their products more widely and using more sophisticated marketing and distribution techniques. Designs that had once been distinctly provincial or regional

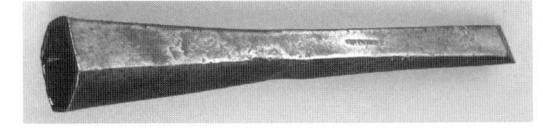

Fig. 20. An hexagonal socket chisel with a very faint mark that possibly reads "BENNET." Bennet was most likely to have been either a London or a Birmingham edge tool maker. OL: 6 7/8". CW 1999-76.

Fig. 21. Detail from Gin Lane *by William Hogarth, 1697-1764; line engraving, England, 1751.*

became accepted as the norm over much larger areas. For all intents and purposes, the result was the establishment of national English tool styles that were distinctly different from those found elsewhere in Europe. The chisels, saws, planes, and bitstocks of the first half of the eighteenth century show what that style entailed.

As with the earlier period, archaeologically recovered tools are important sources of information, but the number of surviving tools from this period, while not huge, is vastly greater than for the seventeenth century.

Paring, firmer, and other tanged chisels and gouges are almost triangular in shape, flaring from the bolster in a smooth curve, or re-curve, to the cutting edge (Fig. 19). The wider the cutting edge, the more dramatic is this flare. Socket chisels continue to have hexagonal sockets (Fig. 20). Bevelled-edge chisels, whether tanged or socketed, seem to disappear, aside from a slight break filed along the top edges of the blade to make them easier to handle and more attractive. A number of the surviving chisels bear makers' marks. They almost inevitably are those of Birmingham makers: Moore, Dalaway, Freeth, Allen, Dingley, Parkes.[7]

Few handsaws from this period survive, but trade cards and prints like William Hogarth's *Gin Lane* suggest that the toes of saws often were cut square or slightly rounded and that handles were closed (Fig 21). Based upon the hammered surface of the blade, its shape, and the handle mounting screws, the saw shown in Figure 22 may be one of the earliest English handsaws extant. Because of its amateurish design and execution, the handle does not appear to have been made by a professional toolmaker: I have assumed it is a replacement but the saw could have been purchased unhandled. I do not have any evidence indicating if and until when saws were sold as "handsaw plates," that is, unhandled blades to be handled by their owners regardless of their skill.[8] The blade may well be iron. It is almost surely made of hammered, rather than rolled plate, although iron was being rolled into plates, or sheets, as early as the 1690s,

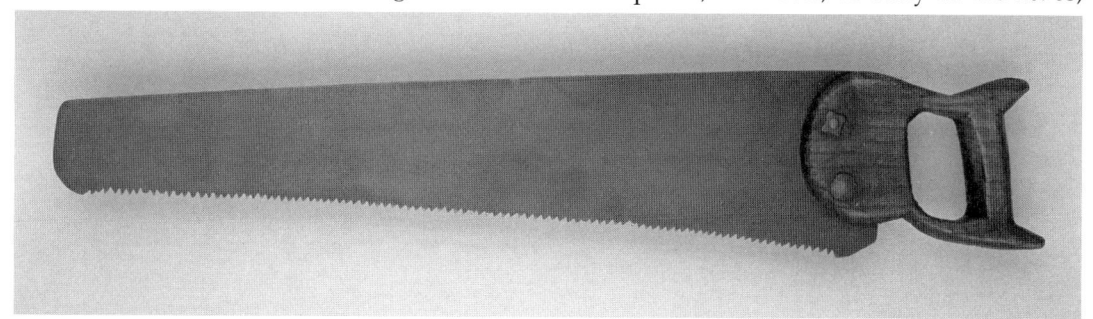

Fig. 22. Handsaw with illegible maker's mark. Possibly seventeenth century. OL: 23 ½". CW 1997-106.

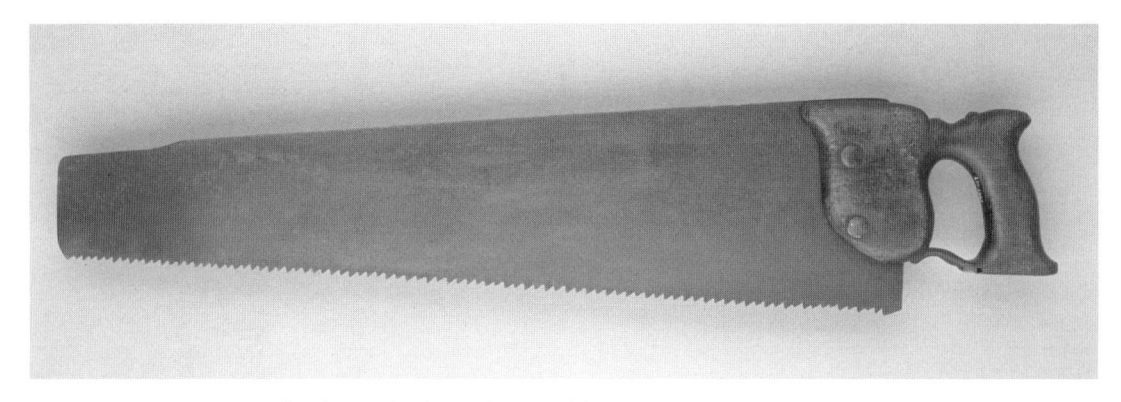

Fig. 23. Handsaw with illegible maker's mark. Probably mid-eighteenth century. Engraved with owner's name "Mickael Hedges". OL: 26 ¼". CW 1997-107.

Fig. 24. Detail of the handle of the saw shown in Fig. 23.

especially in conjunction with the manufacture of tinplate. The iron screws holding the handle onto the blade are large-headed, and the nuts are square, with their sides filed away to create a castellated design.

The handsaw shown in Figure 23 is no doubt later, probably nearer mid-century. It has an illegible maker's mark and is engraved with the name "Mickael Hedges". This blade looks surprising modern with a "notched" toe and the remnants of a nib. The saw also is handled using castellated nuts (Fig. 24). The handle is mounted and shaped in such a way that, if what is left of the blade is about the same width as when it was new, the hand grip lies near what must have been the mid-line of the blade, rather than above it, as with later saws.

Another saw from this period, albeit in attenuated form, survives in the toolkit of a carpenter/joiner named Judah Woodruff who worked in Farmington, Connecticut, during the 1760s and 1770s (Fig. 25). This saw is stamped "WILLIAM SMITH," who is documented as working in Birmingham from 1718 to 1750.[9] Like the Hedges saw, this one has a flat-bottomed handle and an ogee moulding and a small vestigial scroll on the handle top.

I do not know when backed saws first came into use. There is documentation of two "tenant saws" imported into Virginia from

Fig. 25. Handsaw made by William Smith (1718-1750) of Birmingham and used by Judah Woodruff to build a meetinghouse and residences in Farmington, Connecticutt, during the second half of the century. OL: 16 ¾". Courtesy of the Stanley-Whitman House, Farmington, Connecticut, 417d.

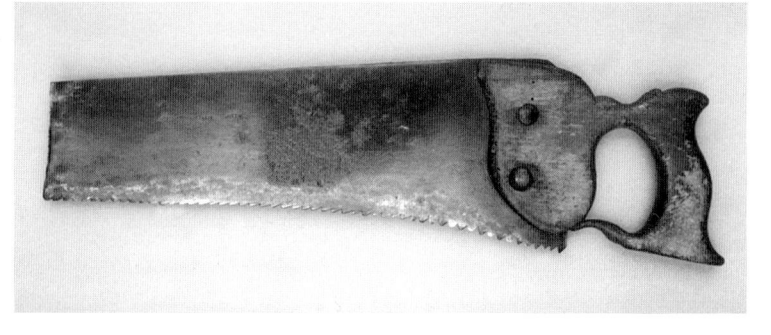

Fig. 26. Backsaw made by "WHITE." Also from the Judah Woodruff tool group. OL: 23¼" Courtesy of the Stanley-Whitman House, Farmington, Connecticut, 417c.

England in 1619[10] A couple more appear in seventeenth-century Virginia probate inventories. Moxon appears to contradict himself in defining a "tenant" saw, or possibly, that term applied to both a framed saw and to an open saw, that "being thin, hath a Back to keep it from bending".[11] By 1708, the probate inventory of Philadelphia joiner Charles Plumley includes "5 handsaws, 4 Tennant Saws, 3 beam saws, 3 small saws", and "1 saw plate."[12] The handsaws average out to about 67 pence, the tenant saws to about 50 pence, the beam to 26 pence, the small to 12 pence, and the saw plate to 10 pence. While this is not conclusive, it suggests that the tenant saws were likely more than wooden-framed webs. It is probable that, at least by the late seventeenth century, what they called a tenant saw is the same thing we mean by that term today, i.e. a saw with a reinforcing back.

The earliest surviving English backsaw I know of is shown in Figure 26. It also is from the Woodruff tool group. It is marked "WHITE," who is thought be to a London maker, and whose saws were highly respected during the period. They were one of the few tools that colonial Americans constantly ordered by maker's name.

This saw definitely looks English, but, again, some details differ from those of later saws. The iron back is very light, and is filed at the toe into another of those vestigial scrolls. The handle is mounted at the blade's centre, leaving the back and a bit of the blade itself uncovered. The handle is closed and has, again, several suggestions of scrolls, with an especially engaging one on the lower strap.

The form of braces remained much the same, and probably most of them continued to be made by their users (Fig. 27). Their bits were still of the flat-tanged variety that could be securely mounted into a wooden pad, which, in turn, could be interchangeably mounted in the wooden bitstock itself (Fig. 28) A significant

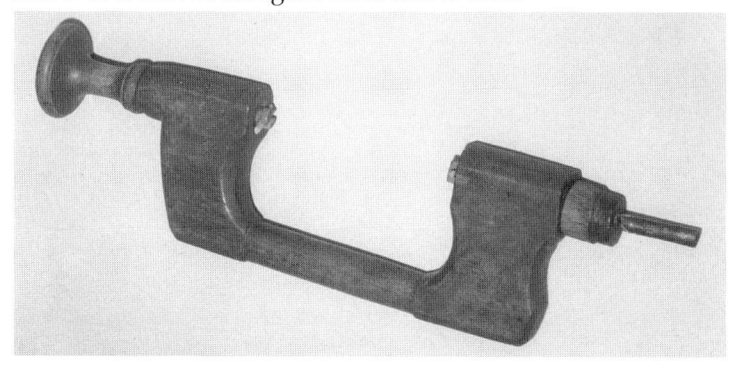

Fig. 27. Bitstock probably made by Thomas Nixon of Framingham, Massachusetts, during the last quarter of the eighteenth century. OL: 17½". Courtesy of the Framingham Historical Society and Museum, Framingham, Massachusetts

Fig. 28. Flat-tang centre bit, marked "FREETH" and made and/or sold by Benjamin Freeth of Birmingham, mid-eighteenth to early nineteenth century. OL: 4 5/8", cutting diameter 5/8". Collection of the Mercer Museum of the Bucks County Historical Society, Doylestown, Pennsylvania, 15228.

innovation, however, was the development of the center bit, first mentioned in that same 1708 Philadelphia inventory of Charles Plumley.

And planes were evolving, both moulding and bench planes. No identified bench planes from this period survive, but a panel raising plane by Robert Wooding illustrates the trend (Fig. 29).

All in all many English tools from this period forward not only have shared specific design details that set them apart, but also share a less definable, but nevertheless real common character that distinguishes them from tools made elsewhere. The approach to tool design

Fig. 29. Panel-raising plane by Robert Wooding, London, 1706-1739. OL: 8 9/16". CW 1986-130.

Fig. 30. The Carpenter's Shop at Forty Hill, Enfield, ca. 1813, by John Hill (1779-1841), oil on canvas, England. Courtesy of the Trustees of the Tate Gallery, Millbank, London.

Fig. 31. English joiners, painted in 1816 by George Forster (?-1842), oil on canvas. Courtesy of the private collection of Barry and Carol Eisenberg, in memory of Bernard H. Taff.

was a functional one. Overall forms and components are generally clean and well proportioned. There is little superfluous decoration, and what there is often was intended not only to improve a tool's aesthetic appeal, but also to make it easier to use or less costly to manufacture. In the main, these tools remained technically similar to those used by other western Europeans, but the reasons why, for example, the English preferred and continued to develop hand- and backsaws rather than narrow-bladed framed saws as on the Continent can only be a matter of conjecture. Was it because of the quality of English steel? The price of that steel? The affluence of English woodworkers compared to those on the Continent?

Another aspect of tool use also had evolved. It is during this period that the range of tools an English or Anglo-American carpenter, joiner, or cabinetmaker was likely to own become fairly standardized. Although the exact composition of kits varied with nearly everyone who practised one of these trades, they had many common components. The 1708 Philadelphia inventory, a 1768 store order from Virginia for a set of joiner's tools,[13] and the inventory Benjamin Seaton took of his chest of tools almost thirty years later all bear a striking resemblance in terms of both the tools they contained and what they were called. Tool types as well as tool nomenclature were becoming standardized.

It is also from this period that the earliest almost complete kits of tools survive.

While a national English tool style appears to have emerged during the latter part of the seventeenth century, the second half of the eighteenth century – especially the years from about 1750 to 1780 – witnessed significant evolutions in tool types, often in the form of standardization, expansion of specialized types, technical improvements, and aesthetic niceties. Again, we have artistic evidence. John Hill's ca. 1813 painting of *The Carpenter's Shop at Forty Hill, Enfield* shows the same types of tools we've been looking at, but their details appear even more modern (Fig. 30). The same is true of George Forster's 1816 painting of a country joiners' shop (Fig. 31). In addition, the number of surviving tools increases dramatically. Benchmarks like the Hewlett gentleman's tool chest that was sold in London on February 13, 1773 (Fig. 32), and the Benjamin Seaton tools that were purchased on December 15, 1796, give us much more exact information about the details of tools than from any previous period. The art and tools themselves also are accompanied by a vastly expanded range of documentary sources: encyclopedias, books intended for use by artisans, catalogues and pattern books, newspaper advertisements, and an ever- increasing volume of business and personal papers, from merchants' records to artisans' estate inventories.

Nearly all the tool forms we have been examining changed during this period. A new pattern of tanged chisels and gouges appears (Fig. 33). The gentle curves of the earlier tools give way to blades that have a distinct shank that flares from the octagonal bolster to the base of the blade and then, softly, takes a turn to form the blade itself. Blades of all but the narrowest chisels and gouges continue to gently flare. Apparently no bevelled-edge chisels were being made. Instead, chisels continued to taper from their bolsters to very thin edges that allowed them

Fig. 32. Gentleman's tool chest and tools sold by London ironmonger William Hewlett on February 13, 1773. OL: 24". CW 1957-123.

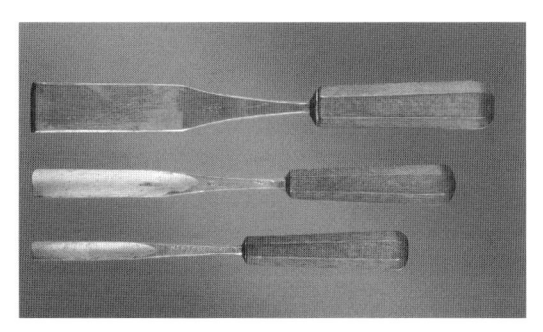

Fig. 33. Gouges and chisel from the Hewlett gentleman's tool chest. They were made and/or sold by Thomas Newbould of Sheffield, and marked "BEST." Chisel OL: 12" CW1957-123, A8, A7, A9.

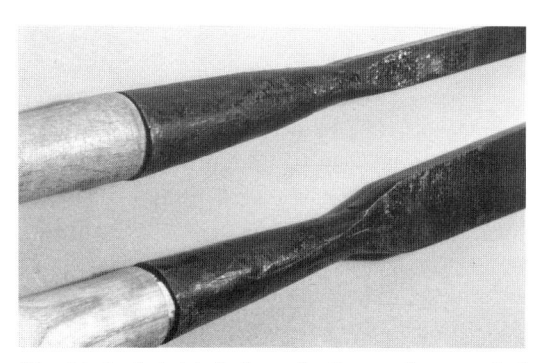

Fig. 34. Socket chisels from the Seaton chest marked by Sheffield makers "P. LAW" and "MITCHELL". Courtesy of the Guildhall Museum, Rochester, Kent.

to work in tight corners. The sockets of socket chisels and gouges changed from the hexagonal ones that were in vogue for at least a hundred years to round ones (Fig. 34).

Both of these changes in design occur about the same time, in the late 1760s or early 1770s, and as England's edge tool industry is being transferred from London and Birmingham to Sheffield. These new-design tools almost always are marked with names of Sheffield makers: Law, Newbould, Green, Weldon, Gillot, Bishop.[14] One of the more tantalizing questions that arises in studying eighteenth-century tools is what aspects of Sheffield technology or trade practices stimulated these design changes?

With the exception of some smaller tools, most edge tools continued to be made, as they had been for centuries, by laminating a steel cutting edge onto a wrought-iron body. For most of the eighteenth century, the steel was either some form of cementation steel made by baking wrought iron in the presence of charcoal so that the iron absorbed carbon into its surface, or so-called "German steel" made in a process that involved the direct conversion of pig iron into steel. These traditional steels came in a variety of qualities, but none had consistent carbon content throughout.

In the 1740s Benjamin Huntsman, a Doncaster clockmaker, developed a process to create highly homogenized steel. He did so by melting cementation steel along with a flux in a crucible. When it was in a liquid form, it was poured from the crucible into moulds. Because of this process, it was called "cast steel." This raw material was then forged into the desired

Fig. 35. Cast steel chisels from the Benjamin Seaton chest marked "T. SHAW". Courtesy of the Guildhall Museum, Rochester, Kent.

shape by the same techniques used with any other steel. Good cast steel is an excellent material for making many types of tools.

Although Sheffield became justifiably renown for its cast steel tools during the nineteenth century, its toolmakers took some time to begin using the material. Cast steel is "hot short:" if heated to "normal" iron-to-steel welding temperature, the cast steel crumbles. Sheffield cutlers and toolmakers did not solve the problem of welding cast steel and wrought iron until very late in the eighteenth century, and in the meantime continued to use the older forms of steel. This did not deter them, however, from making certain types of small tools, like the bench chisels in the Seaton chest (Fig. 35), wholly from cast steel, and therefore without the need to do any welding. Carving tools also were made of the material. Colonial Williamsburg has a set of joiner's tools brought from London to New York in 1819. It contains a set of carving tools that definitely are pre-1800, possibly as early as the 1760s or 70s. They are marked with the letter "CS" surmounted by a crown. The "CS" on both these chisels, as well as those noted in the Christopher Gabriel inventories, most likely means "cast steel" (Fig. 36).

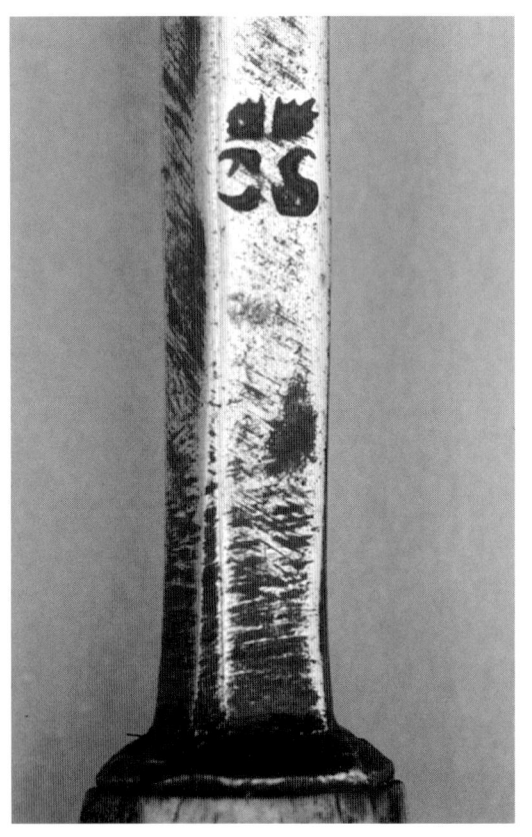

Saws also evolved, both stylistically and technically. Sometime during the third quarter of the century, the old iron screws and castellated nuts were supplanted by brass screws, actually cast-brass bolts with countersunk, flat heads, and slotted cast-brass nuts. This is just one of the indications of the growing availability of brass, a material whose production in England increased dramatically during the eighteenth century. Saw handle forms also evolved (Fig. 37). While retaining round cheeks and a flat-bottomed grip, the decoration at the top of the handle and the form of the lower tongue were simplified.

There is a good probability that the first rolled steel blades were introduced about this time. The English had been plating (hammering steel into sheets) for hundreds of years, and, as mentioned above, sheet iron had been rolled since at least the 1690s. The delay in applying rolling technology to steel may have been the result of a desire to physically consolidate the steel by the pressure of actual hammering, and the rolling technology of the day may not have produced the same results. Whatever the reason, it does not appear that steel was rolled into sheet until the mid-eighteenth century. The first documentation known is in the 1837 Sheffield Directory as quoted in Ken Roberts, *Some 19th Century English Woodworking Tools*: " In 1769 Mr. Thomas Boulsover, the founder of the silver-plated trade, having turned his attention to the manufacture of edge tools &c., built the Whiteley Wood Works, where he established the first machinery for rolling iron and steel into plates, suitable for saws, fenders, spades, shovels, &c., which had

Fig. 36. Carving tool marked with a crown and "CS," most likely indicating that it was made from cast steel. From the George William Cartwright II tool chest. CW G-1986-268, 87; gift of Frank M. Smith.

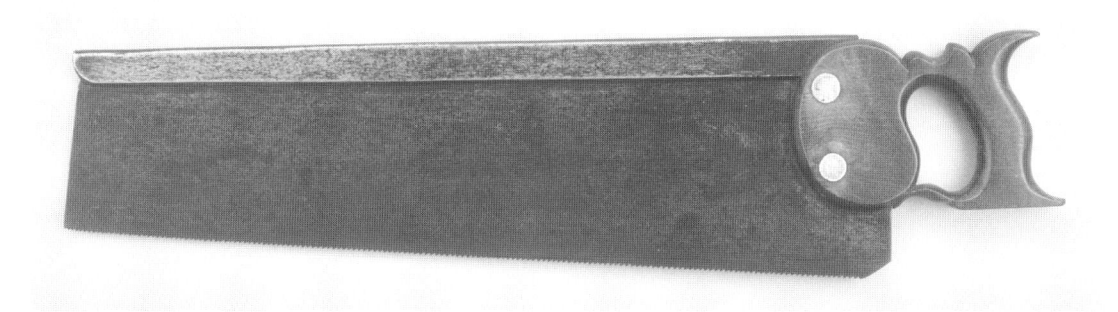

Fig. 37. Tenon saw from the Cartwright tool chest, with an illegible maker's mark, likely dating to the third quarter of the eighteenth century. OL: 23" CW G1986-268, 66; gift of Frank M. Smith.

been previously formed solely by the laborious and more expensive operation of the hammer…"[15]

Interestingly, there is evidence that, while Moxon encourages his readers to purchase saws made of steel rather than hammer-hardened iron, advertisements for saws made of steel in the mid-eighteenth century continue to stress that fact, suggesting that iron saws still were to be had. As late as 1831, the *The Cabinet Cyclopaedia* in its treatise on manufactures in metal notes that "Saws are manufactured either of iron, which is hammer-hardened, or planished on an anvil, to give the requisite degree of stiffness and elasticity; or they are made of shear steel; or, lastly, of cast steel."[16]

It is certain that some late-eighteenth-century saw blades were made of cast steel. Saw blades are made entirely of one material, rather than a welded-together combination of iron and steel. This would have made cast steel a practical saw-making material, and although Gabriel does not note any in his 1791 inventory, cast steel saws are listed in the 1800 inventory, and there is a group of 32 cast steel handsaws that are "country," i.e. likely Sheffield, made.[17]

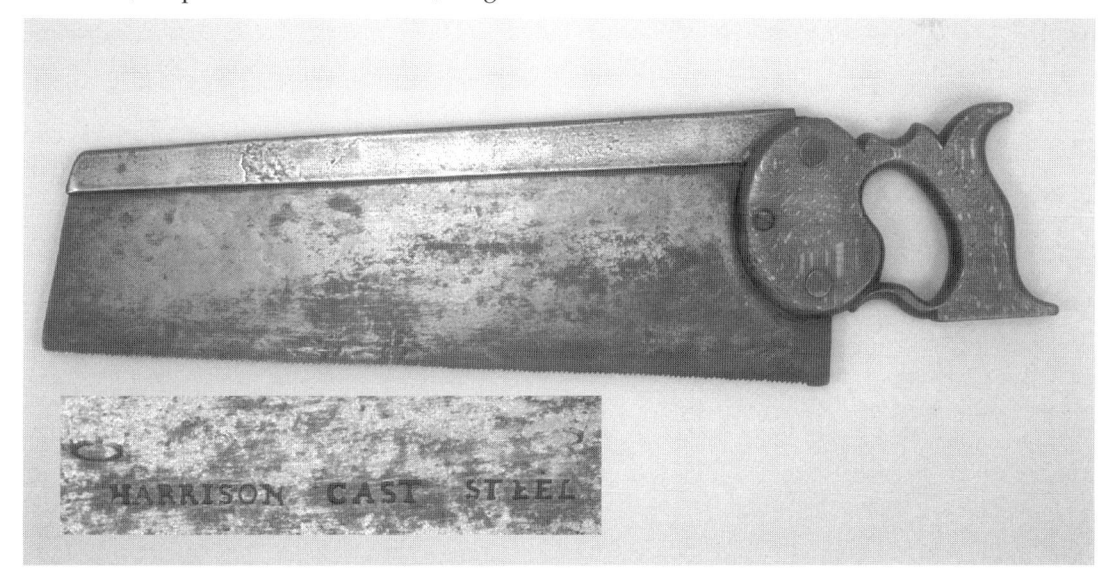

Fig. 38. Tenon saw marked "HARRISON CAST STEEL," with a history of ownership by Samuel Crompton. OL: 20". Courtesy of the Science Museum/Science & Society Picture Library. 1862-8.

Fig. 39. Dovetail saw by Robert or William Dalaway (1746-1809). OL: 15" CW 1990-100.

On the other hand, there is a question about when English woodworking tools were first marked with the words "CAST STEEL". Although there is some evidence suggesting a slightly earlier date for its first appearance, the practice does not become common until after 1800. That creates something of a dilemma when it comes to understanding the Samuel Crompton saw in the Science Museum that Bill Goodman thought was "the earliest known backed saw still in existence".[18] This saw is marked "HARRISON CAST STEEL" (Fig. 38) and has a handle similar to the saw in Figure 37. If the maker is John Harrison and Son of Sheffield, though, then the saw probably dates to no earlier than 1787 and could be as late as 1816. The presence of three crown-shaped marks adjacent to the maker's name suggests an early nineteenth century date.

London remained a centre of saw production through this period. In the first Sheffield directory, dating from 1774, there are four sawmakers listed as such; by 1797, there are 14.[19] Saws continued to be made in Birmingham as well. The dovetail saw in Figure 39, by either Robert or William Dalaway who are

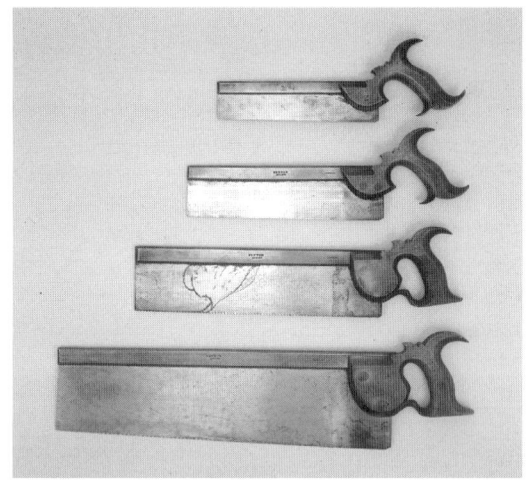

Fig. 41. Backsaws from the Seaton chest, made by John Kenyon of Sheffield. Tenon saw (bottom) OL:23 11/16". Courtesy of the Guildhall Museum, Rochester, Kent.

documented as working from 1746 to 1809, is one of the earliest small backsaws surviving. Its handle is approaching the shape of late-century saws, although it is lighter and more delicate, than, for example, the Kenyon saws in the Seaton chest. It is worth noting that this blade is only about .018 inches thick.

The Kenyon saws in the Seaton chest represent the culmination of saw development during the eighteenth century. The hand- and panel saws are stamped "KENYON," but without an indication of the kind of steel of which they were made (Fig. 40). The blades are broad and boldly curved at the toe and have nibs. The backsaws are brass backed and are

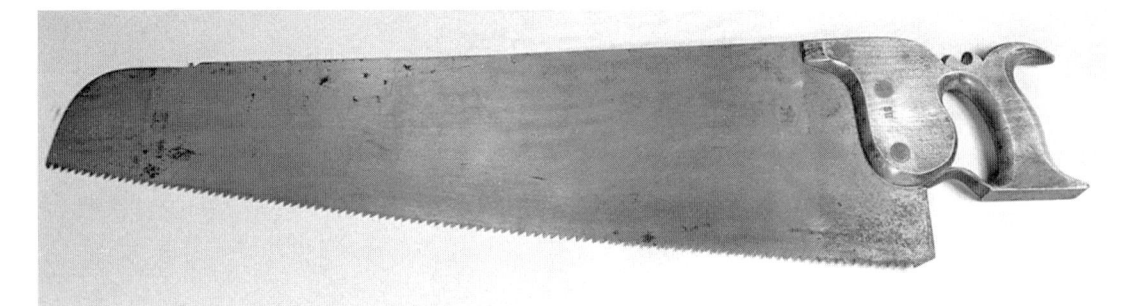

Fig. 40. Hand saw from the Seaton chest, made by John Kenyon of Sheffield. Both the handsaw and the panel saw in the chest have 26-inch blades. Courtesy of the Guildhall Museum, Rochester, Kent.

stamped with the maker's name "KENYON" beneath which is "SPRING" and closer to the handle "LONDON" (Fig. 41). The saws were made in Sheffield and the material is London Spring steel, but there may have been a conscious effort to confuse the material name with the manufacturing location. As early as 1747, Robert Campbell, in his book *The London Tradesman*, suggested the practice: "frequently Cutlers, who have a great Demand for Goods, have them made in the Country, put their own Marks upon them, and sell them for *London* made."[20] These Kenyon backsaws are some of the first English saws of which I know that are marked with the type of steel used in their manufacture, a practice that becomes common in the nineteenth century.

The two larger of the backsaws, the tenon and sash, have closed, flat-bottom handles. The smaller carcass and dovetail saws have open, dolphin-shaped handles. This set gives us a good glimpse of how, by this time, the angles of the handles to the blades' edges vary with the size of the saw, a feature that accommodates for the usual difference in stances the user takes depending upon the operation he is performing – and hence the tool he is using.

Another technical – and marketing – development that occurred during this period was the evolution of the concept of sets, and with it, interchangeability. They are not exactly the same thing, but they are related. Sets of plough plane irons in a range of widths had been available for many years. A technical development in the nature of pads, or chucks, on bitstocks allowed a comparable development in boring tools.

George Washington, the American general and president, long before he became either, decided to remodel his home at Mount Vernon. In 1759 he ordered tools from London for that purpose. Included in the order was a request for "1 Spring Brase

Fig. 42. Two braces with iron pads, the left with a thumbscrew to secure the bit, the right with a button-operated pawl. Both pads are marked "RYLEY" and were made by the Birmingham maker John Ryley (1770-1781). The left stock is oak and homemade. The right is walnut and probably professionally made. OL: 14 5/8" and 14 ¾". CW 1991-99 and 1991-154.

and Bits Compleate".[21] This is the earliest mention of a metal-pad brace known. John Wyke shows such a pad in his catalogue of Lancashire clock and watchmaker's tools on a sheet first published about 1770.[22] These earliest pads were made of iron, and it is likely they had rectangular slots to receive the traditional flat-tanged bits originally designed to be fitted into wooden pads. A thumbscrew held the bit in place (Fig. 42). Soon the pads and bit tangs were modified so that the pad had a tapering square slot to receive a corresponding tapering square bit tang. A spring detent, released by a push button, held the bit in place. Just about any bit would fit – more or less – into any pad, although bits were fitted to a particular brace by filing a notch in their tangs to receive the detent.

These iron pads evolved through several different designs and then were replaced by pads made of cast brass. This innovation, like so many others, probably was driven by several factors. Brass was more readily available than previously, it was a flashier material, and, possibly most importantly, it was easier to cast and finish pads of brass in quantity than to forge them of iron. By the 1790s, planemakers like George Mutter were selling brass-pad braces with sets of bits.

The history and development of planes during the eighteenth century is well documented by a number of researchers and writers. The evolution of moulding plane designs is well defined (Fig. 43), but planes also illustrate a number of trends seen in other tools. By about 1770, their designs became almost rigidly standardized. There are technical innovations, most notably the invention of the double iron. Bench planes, once frequently made by the user himself, became readily available commercial products. Cast-brass elements became common on the more complex planes. Planemakers and tool dealers offered planes in sets of size and shape ranges.

What is encouraging this standardization and ever-growing commercial availability of tools of ever-expanding variety? The answer is a book that has yet to be written. There would

Fig. 43. Molding plane evolution during the eighteenth century. Top to bottom: ovolo by Robert Wooding, ca. 1705, OL: 10 3/8"; number 16 hollow by John Cogdell, mid-eighteenth century; number 12 hollow by John Sym, late eighteenth century; number 12 hollow by John Lund, ca. 1820. All are London makers. CW 1986-34; 1982-223; 1991-619, 2; 1952-277, 49.

be a host of questions included, but many of the major factors that nourished the emergence of national tool styles during the late seventeenth century became only more powerful over the next hundred years: a market that dramatically expanded, both domestically but even more so, in overseas colonies and trading partners. Improvements in internal transportation allowed inland manufacturers to ship their goods far more readily and less expensively, and British overseas shipping continued to be relatively inexpensive, especially compared to the costs of inland shipping in places like America.

The chief tool manufacturing centres of London, Birmingham, Sheffield, and Lancashire responded to the increased demand and the nature of far-flung markets in a number of ways: Each of these centres focussed on the production of particular tool types: Lancashire on watch, clock, and other precision tools; Birmingham on large and small iron and steel tools and rules, while the light edge-tool industry, once prominent there, gradually moved to Sheffield during the last quarter of the century. London was known for planes, saws and carving tools. Possibly as a result of these concentrations of production, new technologies emerged, there was a cross-pollination of technologies, and makers explored the application of new materials.

Tool merchant/manufacturers organized their production so that it was undertaken by a series of highly specialised tradesmen – even more specialised than before. This improved the efficiency of manufacturing as well as, in many cases, the quality of the product. Most of these individuals producers worked on the putting-out (out-working) system. They maintained their own small shops and worked for a master who supplied them with materials and payment at a piece rate. The masters also

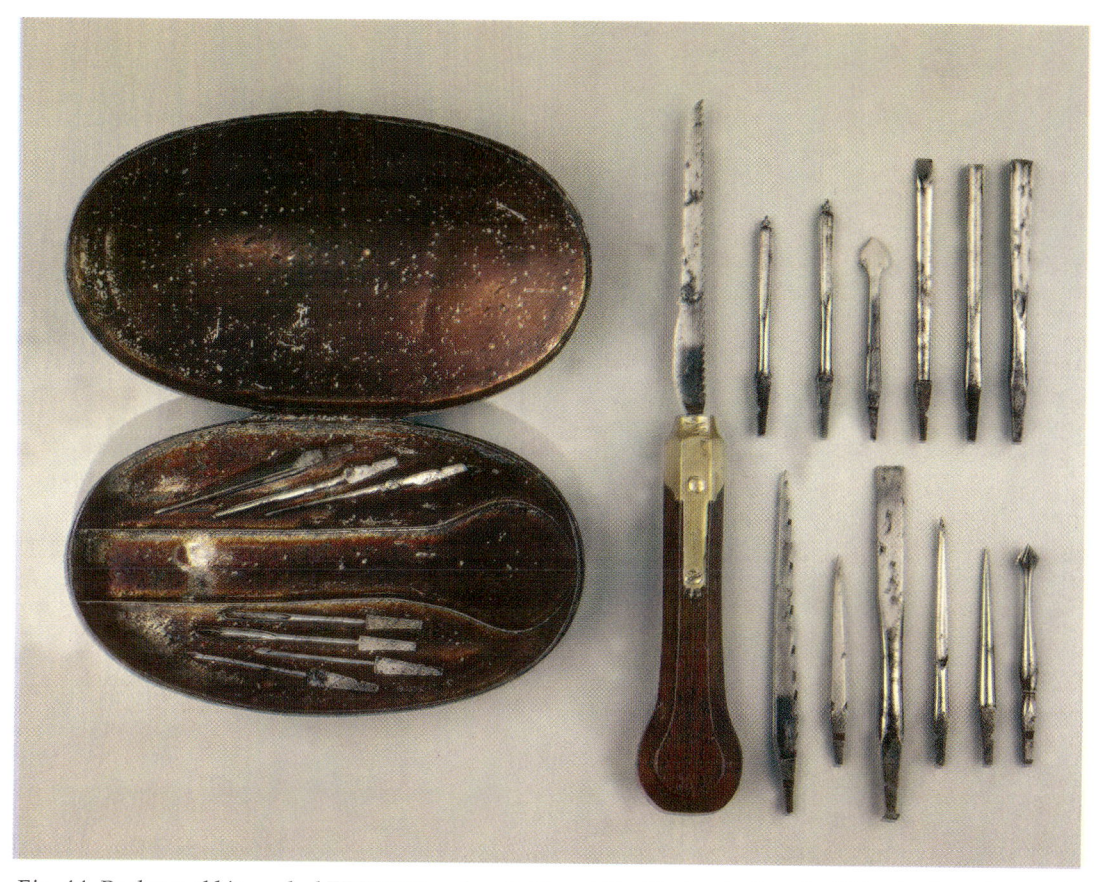

Fig. 44. Pocket tool kit marked FREETH and probably sold by Benjamin Freeth of Birmingham during the early nineteenth century. Handle with saw OL: 10 5/8" CW 1991-459, acquired through the generosity of Sharon and James W. Swinehart.

available carving tools to tools for fretwork, marquetry, and veneers. Even a preference for the decreasing size of dovetails used in cabinet work demanded the refinement of backsaws.

Once toolmaking and marketing took off, it led to the vicious circle with which we are so familiar today. Not only did toolmakers seek to meet existing demand, they sought to increase that demand. Fancier tools; tools manufactured in overt ranges of quality from common to best; tools in sets; tool kits, like chests of gentlemen's tools; novelty tools like pocket sets (Fig. 44) all were, at least in part, efforts on the part of tool makers and merchants to expand the markets for their products. That trend continued to accelerate, first with English toolmakers and then at a frenzied pace with American inventors and toolmakers throughout the nineteenth century.

By 1810, a definably English approach to

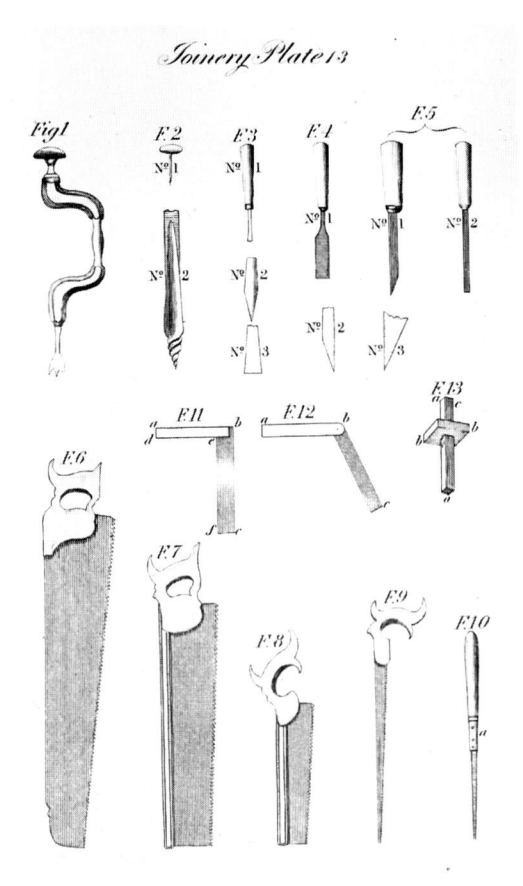

Fig. 45. "Joinery Plate 13" from Peter Nicholson, Mechanical Exercises *(London, J. Taylor, 1812).*

supplied the patterns to which the tools were to be made. This trend resulted in more standardized tools, as did the practice of selling them to distant markets using either samples or printed catalogues. The first illustrated English catalogue was one of clock and watch tools, published by John Wyke of Liverpool beginning in 1758. Birmingham followed during the late eighteenth century. The earliest Sheffield catalogue may have predated Smith's *Key to the Manufactories of Sheffield*, but the *Key*, printed in 1816, is the first well-known depiction of Sheffield tools.[23]

Along with economic and organizational factors, new types of products stimulated new tool types and designs. Changing tastes in architecture and furniture stimulated the refinement of tools ranging from commercially

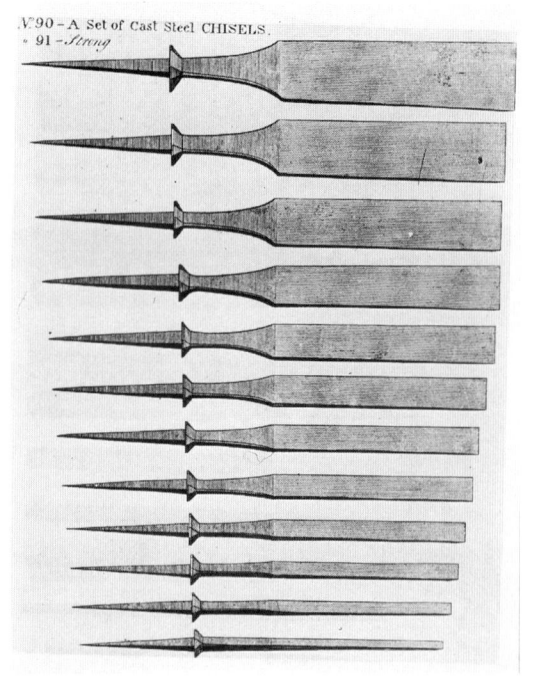

Fig. 46. "A Set of Cast Steel CHISELS," from Joseph Smith, Explanation or Key, to the Various Manufactories of Sheffield *(Sheffield: Joseph Smith, 1816). Courtesy of Local Studies, Sheffield Libraries, Archives and Information.*

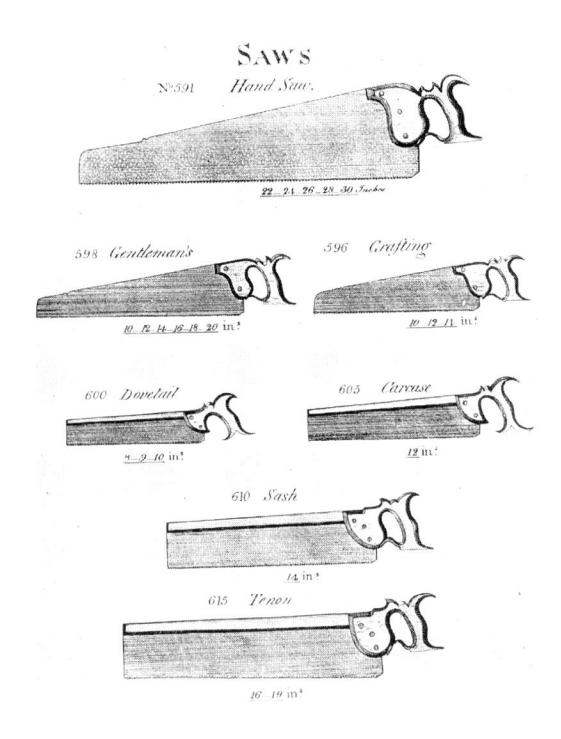

Fig. 47. 'Saws" from Smith's Key. *Courtesy of Courtesy of Local Studies, Sheffield Libraries, Archives and Information.*

tool design and tool making was well established, and many tools had achieved their "modern" form (Fig. 45). Nearly every tool type, even those once almost always homemade, was available from commercial sources. To be sure, as new technologies emerged, some tools continued to evolve. Iron braces, with a variety of chuck types, become more common. Iron and brass planes were manufactured. Most of those developments make sense but a couple raise some question.

By the time Smith's *Key* was published, tanged chisels have changed shape once again. Bolsters are generally smaller. The blade shanks form a harder shoulder where they transition into the blade proper, and all but the widest blades, if they flare at all, do so only slightly (Fig. 46). By the 1830s or 40s, these shoulders become even more acute and blades are made parallel in width throughout their length.

Handsaw toes remain rounded at their tops, but the curve transitions into a vertical end. The notch and nib persist (Fig. 47). Backsaws blades seem to be more intentionally tapered. While from the earliest known backed saws on, blades taper toward the toe, the degree of this taper varies. Blades are held in their backs by friction, and the exact degree of taper may have resulted from the process of fitting the backs and trueing the blades. But in the 1810s, many backsaws take on a much more exaggerated and apparently intentional taper.

What is driving these changes? Is it new manufacturing methods? Designs that save time or materials? The changing role of hand tools in the face of the introduction of power tools? Or the changing tastes in tool design itself?

I think that sometimes we underrate the impact that philosophical bents and artistic tastes have had on traditional tool design. The artisans who used these tools were quite aware of changing tastes. Many of their products were constantly undergoing redesigns or tweaks to make them more tasteful and therefore more

> WANTS Employment, and is now at Leisure, a Master Workman in the various Branches of the Cabinet Busineſs, chineſe, gotick, carving, and turning; is well acquainted with the Theory and Practice in any of the grand Branches of the five ancient Orders, *viz.* Ornamental Architects, gothick, chineſe, and modern Taſte, *&c* alſo Colonades, Porticoes, Frontiſpieces, *&c.* to Doors; compound, pick Pediment, and plain Tabernacle Chimney Pieces; chineſe, ramp, and twiſt Pedeſtals; geometrical, circular, plain, and common Stair Caſes, and ſundry other Pieces of Architect too tedious mentioning. My chief Deſire is to act in the Capacity of Superintender, or Superviſor, over any reaſonable Number of Hands, either in public or private Buildings. I have an elegant Aſſortment of Tools, and Books of Architect, which I imported from *London* and *Liverpool.*
> (2‖)   MARDUM V. EVENGTON.
> N. B.   I am at preſent at Capt. *Richard Baugh's,* in *Cheſterfield,* near *Bermuda* and *Shirley Hundreds.*

Fig. 48. Advertisement of Mardun V. Eventon placed in the Williamsburg *Virginia Gazette for August 22, 1777.*

Fig. 49. Handsaw with walnut handle carved with the arms of the Carpenters' Company and dated 1696. Courtesy of Norman P. Nilsson. Photograph by Ted Ingraham.

marketable. A cabinetmaker in Virginia, looking for work in 1777 and trying to establish his credentials as knowledgeable, skilled, and up-to-date, advertised, "I have an elegant Assortment of Tools, and Books of Architecture, which I imported from *London* and *Liverpool*" (Fig. 48). Did ownership of the highest quality and most modern tools at least sometimes imply that their owner was himself an artisan of both taste and capability? Did toolmakers also do their best to make tools that, even in what we think of as the slow-paced, pre-industrial world, were up-to-date and modern?

I think so, and it became more important as time went on. The first tools we looked at were very organic in form. It is almost as if their elements grew – like a plant – to their final shape. They are generally symmetrical, but in a loose, natural way. Filed and carved suggestions of scrolls again recall natural elements.

The remnant of a handsaw, dated 1696, is probably the earliest datable English handsaw surviving (Fig. 49). The handle, almost without a doubt, was made by the saw's owner. It could have replaced a commercially made handle, or it could be a handle installed on a blade sold without one. Incorporated within the foliage and scrolls of the handle are the owner's initials, the date, and the arms of the Carpenters' Company. There is no doubt this is an English saw, but the overall effect is very reminiscent of the much more stylized carving on totes and throats of very early Dutch bench planes. This saw handle draws the inspiration for its decoration from the baroque style popular in Europe during the seventeenth century.

By the time of the White tennon saw, shown in Figure 26, baroque elements remain, but the handle design is much more rococo, consisting of smooth curves terminating in vestigial scrolls. This saw was made at the height of the popularity of the rococo style in England.

Moving on to the Seaton saws shown in Figures 40 and 41, the handles are plainly straightforward, with well articulated flats and curves and much simpler decorative elements. They reflect well the taste for clean line and curve so important in the neoclassical style.

A similar change can be seen in the chamfering of moulding planes. The mid-seventeenth century plane in Figure 15 has its chamfers and shoulder stopped using an architectural approach. Gradually – or maybe suddenly – this laborious detail gave way to a much less bold gouge cut or lamb's tongue. This, and the narrowing of chamfers, saved time and effort for the planemaker. It also transformed the tool from a very baroque style to a lighter, more delicate, and hence, more fashionable one. A few years ago, Colonial Williamsburg acquired the plane shown in Figure 50 decorated with both an architecturally stopped shoulder and, within that, a lamb's tongue. Whether this is a transitional piece, or simply evidence of a highly motivated planemaker of later date remains to be determined.

Along the same lines (as several researchers have suggested) it is likely that one of the impetuses for the evolution of moulding plane wedge finials from essentially a round to an elliptical shape is the transition of preference for Roman mouldings, based upon arcs of circles, to a preference for Grecian mouldings based upon arcs of ellipses.

Another design trend that manifests itself

Fig. 50. Early English ovolo plane, beech, maker unknown, with later iron. OL: 10 ¾". CW 1989-386.

over these couple hundred years is a slow, if constant, drive toward precision. The old, loose, organic forms gave way to much more precisely made tools. I have often wondered if the flaring blades of those beautiful mid-eighteenth century Birmingham chisels or even of their slightly less organic Sheffield successors gave way to the rigid – and in my eyes, by comparison – much less attractive blades of the 1810s and 20s because both toolmakers and tool users all of a sudden found it quite intolerable to make, buy, or use a chisel that with each sharpening changed its width. In this day and age, a ½" chisel should always be a ½" chisel!

References

1. An exhibition about eighteenth-century Anglo-American woodworking tools and their production, acquisition, use, and significance as historical artifacts presented at Colonial Williamsburg's DeWitt Wallace Decorative Arts Museum, Williamsburg, Virginia, 1994-1995.
2. Joseph Moxon, *Mechanick Exercises, or the Doctrine of Handy-Works*, London, 1703 ed. Reprinted by The Astragal Press, Morristown, NJ, 1989.
3. Randle Holme, in his *Academy of Armory* (Chester, 1688), describes and illustrates a vast number of everyday objects employed as heraldic symbols. Among them are many trade tools. The text and drawings, including additional material from the original archive, are available on a CD-ROM published by the British Library, titled *Living and Working in 17th Century England*.
4. André Félibien, *Des Principes de l'Architecture, de la Sculpture, de la Peinture, et des autres Arts qui en Dependent. Avec un Dictionnaire des Termes propres à chacun de ces Arts*, Paris, 1676.
5. Jane and Mark Rees, ed. *British Planemakers from 1700*, 3rd ed. Needham Market, 1993, p. 4.
6. W. L. Goodman, *The History of Woodworking Tools*, London, 1964, p. 149, Fig. 151.
7. Robert Moore (father and son, ca. 1700-1776), Robert or William Dalaway (1746-1809), Samuel and Sampson Freeth (1767-1776), John Allen (1767-1791), Edward, Richard (son), and Richard (grandson) Dingley (1725-1805), Isaac Parkes (1754-?). I thank Don and Anne Wing for providing me with current information regarding some of these makers. Their research, some of whcih they publish in *Early Planemakers of London* …(Marion, Massachusetts, 2005), is significantly expanding our knowledge about early edge-tool makers.
8. The 1649 inventory of the estate of Governor John Winthrop of Massachusetts includes "three joiners' saw plates." A. B. Forbes, ed., John Winthrop, *Winthrop Papers V, 1645-1649*, Boston, 1929-1947.pp. 333-336, as referenced by Paul B. Kebabian in "Eighteenth-Century American Toolmaking," *Eighteenth-Century Woodworking Tools: Papers Presented at a Tool Symposium, May 19-22, 1994*, James M. Gaynor, ed., Williamsburg, 1997.
9. Dates given for tool makers are derived from a variety of primary sources, principally trades directories. They represent documented dates but not necessarily an individual's entire period of work.
10. "The Cost of Furnishing the *Margaret*", July-September 1619, transcribed in Susan M. Kingsbury, *The Records of the Virginia Company of London*, Washington, 1933, Vol. 3, pp. 178-179.
11. Joseph Moxon, *op. cit.* p. 103.
12. Plumley inventory as quoted in Benno M. Forman, *American Seating Furniture*, New York, 1988, p. 371-2
13. Illustrated in James M. Gaynor and Nancy L. Hagedorn, *Tools: Working Wood in Eighteenth-Century America,* Williamsburg, 1993, p. 26.
14. Philip Law (1773-1856), Thomas and Samuel Newbould (1773-1797), John Green and succcessors (1774-1821), William Weldon (1774-1787), Malin Gillot (1774-

1797). Little is known about Bishop but he is thought to be a Sheffield maker.
15. Kenneth D. Roberts, *Some 19th Century English Woodworking Tools,* Fitzwilliam, NH, 1980, p. 10.
16. Rev. Dionysius Lardner, *The Cabinet Cyclopaedia: Useful Arts: A Treatise on the Progressive Improvement and Present State of the Manufactures in Metal. Volume I. Iron and Steel*, London, 1831, p. 333. This treatise, along with information about steels contained in Frederick Overman, *The Manufacture of Steel,* Philadelphia, 1851, and in H. R. Schubert, *History of The British Iron and Steel Industry from c. 450 B.C. to A.D. 1775* (London, 1957), were brought to my attention by Kenneth Schwarz, Colonial Williamsburg Historic Trades master blacksmith. All of these works shed interesting light on the nature of period steels and their use in manufacturing.
17. Jane and Mark Rees, *Christopher Gabriel and the Tool Trade in 18th century London*, Needham Market, 1997
18. Goodman, *op. cit.* p. 149.
19. *Sketchley's Sheffield Directory,* Bristol, 1774 and *A Directory of Sheffield*, Sheffield, 1787, the latter reprinted by TATHS, 2004.
20. Robert Campbell, *The London Tradesman,* London, 1747, p. 239
21. John C. Fitzpatrick, ed., *The Writings of George Washington from the Original Manuscript Sources 1745-1799, Volume 2, 1757-1769*, Washington, 1931, pp. 327-336.
22. Alan Smith, ed., *A Catalogue of Tools for Watch and Clock Makers by John Wyke of Liverpool*, reprint of the original in the Winterthur Museum Library, Charlottesville, 1978, plate 35. Ted Crom discusses John Wyke and his business in detail in *Trade Catalogues 1542-1842*, Melrose, Florida, 1989.
23. Joseph Smith, *Explanation or Key to the Various Manufactories of Sheffield,* Sheffield, 1816. Reprinted by the Early American Industries Association, 1975. Introduction by John Kebabian.

Acknowledgements
Thanks to Nancy Hagedorn, Anne and Don Wing, Jane Rees, Simon Barley, Ken Schwarz, Hans Lorenz, Craig McDougal; to those who have allowed me access to study and publish their tools; and the authors who have preceded me and on whose findings all this is based.

All illustrations are courtesy of the Colonial Williamsburg Foundation, with photography by Hans Lorenz and Craig McDougal, unless noted otherwise.

The author
Jay Gaynor is Director of Historic Trades at the Colonial Williamsburg Foundation in Williamsburg, Virginia. Prior to assuming that position in 2002, he served as the Foundation's Curator of Mechanical Arts, responsible for the tools and implements and other mechanical objects in the Foundation's collections. He curated the 1994 exhibit *Tools: Working Wood in 18th-Century America* and has written and lectured extensively on early tools and trades. He is a founder member of the Tools and Trades History Society and a past president of the Early American Industries Association.

Fig. 1a

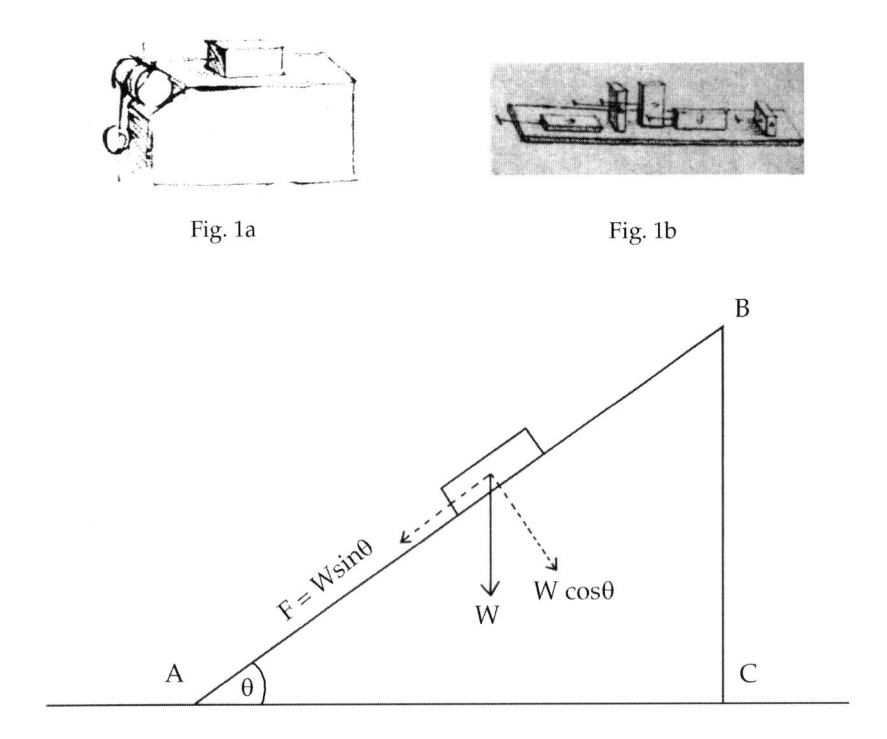

Fig. 1b

Fig. 1c. The inclined plane method.

Fig. 1. The "brick" experiments.

(a) Leonardo's drawing, c.1500, of the first known experiments on friction. A rectangular block, (weight W), with different sized faces is placed on a flat table. A pulley is used to run a string from the block to a balance pan. Weights are added to the pan until the block begins to move. The weight, F, required to cause motion is noted. Increasing the weight of the block required a proportionate increase in the weight, F, to cause movement.

(b) Leonardo observed that F was the same whichever face was in contact with the surface. He showed also that it made no difference if the block was pulled sideways.

(c) A second method, also used by Leonardo, is the inclined plane experiment. A block, as above, on a board is placed on a bench. One end of the board is lifted. The angle θ, at which the block starts to slide is recorded. In this cast, also, the independence on surface area is confirmed, but the method does not lend itself to investigating the effect of weight since the components of force (W) down and into the plane (shown dotted) cancel out.

From (a) and (b), the ratio, F/W is constant for any pair of materials. This is defined as the coefficient of static friction, μ. From (c) it can be shown readily that μ = BC/AC = tan θ. This was established by the Swiss mathematician, L. Euler (1707 – 1783).

The upthrust from the board, equal to the component of weight of the block is not shown.

Science friction, machines, and corrugated planes

Warren Hewertson

The phenomenon of friction is of immense importance in all aspects of life. It is fundamental to animal motion, tools, machines, and transport. On the positive side, friction is essential for anchoring plant roots, walking, pulley belt driving, fire lighting, and vehicle traction, steering, and braking. Its negative aspects include resistance to movement of tools on surfaces, drag losses in transport, and wear between moving parts. Low friction surfaces, e.g. muddy, oily or icy, can have disastrous effects on animal and vehicle locomotion. Whole industries have been built on friction reduction through lubrication and surface modification. In other applications, improved contact or grip, by increasing friction, can be achieved.

This article revisits the characteristics of friction in terms of force and the area and nature of contact between surfaces. An imbalance between the understanding of these developments and the design of various tools is discussed. Particular attention is given to so-called corrugated sole planes. Many splendid pieces were made from the mid-19th century, but few, if any, produced the claimed friction reduction.

Friction is a force of reaction to motion; it is generated when an object resting on a surface is pushed or pulled. Friction acts in a direction opposite to that of the applied force. If the resistance is greater than the applied force, of course no movement occurs. This is called static friction and it is seen when, for example, a box rests on a slope, whereas a ball would roll down it. If the applied force is high enough to overcome frictional resistance (e.g. the angle of a slope is increased) the box will move. This is termed dynamic (or kinetic) friction.

Historical background

Man found ways of overcoming friction with lubricants (e.g. water, animal fats) or rollers as early as 5,000 BC. The nature of friction as a resistance opposing sliding/rolling motion was recorded by Aristotle (*c.* 500 BC). The Vikings used fish oil lubricants to aid dragging small ships over a causeway in Scotland *c.* 800 AD. (This was a short cut to the Atlantic Ocean).

When the engineer G. Amontons presented his two "laws" of friction to the French Academy in 1699 it was not realised that he had been anticipated by Leonardo da Vinci by about 200 years. Leonardo showed, by two series of elegantly simple experiments, that, firstly, friction, F, is directly proportional to the weight, W, of an object on a flat surface, and secondly, that friction is quite independent of surface area for a given weight. The ratio of F to W was called the coefficient of friction, μ (Fig. 1).

Unfortunately, Leonardo's major notes on science and engineering did not surface in public until about 1890. Meanwhile, the French Academy[1] accepted Amonton's first "law" as obvious, but questioned the validity of the second. In 1781, C.A. Coloumb, the French scientist famous for his studies of electricity, confirmed the Leonardo/Amontons findings; he suggested that the main cause of friction was the strong resistance to movement caused by interlocking of surface peaks and troughs.[2,3] The "brick" experiments are, to this day, widely demonstrated in introductory mechanics.

Coulomb also showed that static friction is greater than dynamic friction (Fig. 2). These investigations demonstrated further that for solid/solid sliding friction, the coefficient of friction is almost constant with speed. This, of course, is not the case with solid/gas and solid/liquid systems due to turbulence losses with increasing speed.

Sometimes a new ship on its slipway fails to launch when the restraints have been removed. This arises because of a "bedding in"

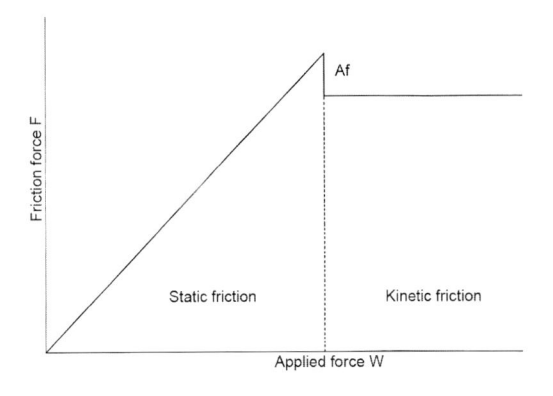

Fig. 2. Static and dynamic friction. The force is increased until the body begins to slide; the resistance falls to the level of dynamic friction. Af is

caused by the increasing weight of the ship, as it is constructed, on the slipway. Increased force, in addition to that of the inclined plane, is required to move the structure down the slipway (Fig. 2).

So, the important aspects causing friction between two surfaces are the forces pushing them together – usually weight – and the nature of the two objects themselves. The latter gives rise to the value of the coefficient of friction, μ. The independence from surface area is apparent if one thinks of a heavy doorstop; it is equally effective whether standing on three legs or a large flat base. Similarly, a towel resting unevenly on a rail is not supported any better by a 50 mm diameter tube than a 5 mm rod. Of course the pressure will vary, but the weight to be moved is constant. Perhaps the most dramatic illustration of this point is the phenomenal traction developed by a heavy locomotive through an extremely small area of contact between driving wheels and rails.

Soft surfaces, friction, and lubrication
There are, in fact, some cases where lowering pressure by increasing area (and changing the nature of the surface) are essential to effect sliding. The obvious one is the use of skis – they allow support to enable gliding over snow rather than just sinking into it. The heat generated by sliding friction melts some snow and provides increased lubrication. Similarly, heavy rocks can be dragged over soft ground by distributing the load on a large area pallet. These examples do not defy the second law of friction; they illustrate a change of mechanism from "ploughing" a soft surface to skiing. A hydrofoil at speed on water demonstrates a similar principle; drag is much lower than that of a comparable capacity boat.

Good lubricants have very low coefficients of friction. Examples are lubricating oils having components with heads which stick to a metal surface, and tails which are soluble in oil. Graphite and melting ice have particularly low μ values. Polytetrafluoroethylene (PTFE) has the lowest μ of a man-made material (< 0.1), hence its widespread use in valve lubrication and pan coating. The lowest known μ value is that of synovial fluids found in all animal joints (c. 0.01).

Ball bearings, and even more so, roller bearings, have achieved somewhat lower values of μ than the best bushes (see later). Indeed, modern lubricated ball and roller bearings have frictional properties of the same order as synovial fluids. The most effective way, but not the cheapest, to reduce friction is to reduce the effective mass. Thus a cushion of air on an air hockey table allows the puck to move virtually unimpeded. The inverse, of course, is the Hovercraft, the largest of which can carry thousands of tonnes. Helicopters, gliders, and aircraft can be considered in the same vein. The friction solid/air (drag) is much reduced compared with solid/solid. Recent advances in magnetic levitation technology allow very rapid train transport, by reduction of effective mass to almost zero.

Lubrication between sliding and rolling surfaces is readily achieved by lubricating oils, wax, graphite, and "Molyslip" (molybdenum disulphide), etc. The last two solids are valuable when sticky dirt-attracting oils must be avoided. They are both layered structures where the "flakes" are readily separated and flow over each other with ease. Good liquid lubricants work by the fact that films between the surfaces change the interaction entirely.

Thus, in Figure 3, the coefficient of friction

is not metal-metal but a product of metal/ lubricant − lubricant/lubricant − lubricant/metal. This can reduce frictional losses by orders of magnitude and ensure smooth running of piston engines, for example.

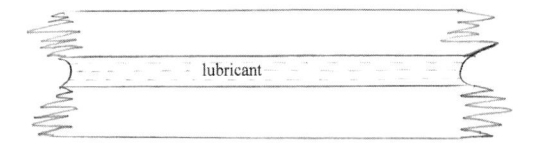

Fig. 3. Thick film lubrication of solid surfaces

Common practice when a considerable thickness of wood has to be removed with a jack plane is to apply wax to the sole. Elegant examples of friction reduction by use of metal oiling planes, which had reservoirs of oil to ports in the sole of the plane, are known from America in the late 19th century.[4] A sharp knife cuts well-oiled leather much more readily than dry leather. The engineering plastic composites, glass-filled PTFE, and PTFE-filled metal sinters, would make excellent low friction soleplates. But it may well be that the time for such technology has passed. Rolling friction is much lower than sliding friction under similar loads. This arises through the fact that rolling involves a continuous movement of bearings away from a surface. Thus wheeled vehicles are much more efficient than sledges – unless the latter are running on ice.

An illustration of the dramatic effect of friction reduction by lubrication is to compare the stopping distances of vehicles in dry, wet, and icy conditions (Table 1).

High friction

Interestingly, µ values greater than 1 are obtained in a number of instances relevant to woodworking and engineering. The energy of interaction between two surfaces is usually dissipated mainly as heat, with a minor proportion lost due to wear. However, the wear component can become the major energy sink between a soft surface sliding over a hard surface. Such examples are the sanding of timber, especially softwoods, grinding of blades (here

Solid/Solid	µ	Stopping Distance (m at 100 km/hr)
Rubber/dry road	0.8	46
Rubber/wet road	0.5	74
Rubber/icy road	0.1	369
Steel/dry rails	0.3	123
Steel/wet rails	0.2	184

Table 1. µ values, after McGraw Hill.[5]

both metal and particles of abrasive are removed), and skidding of rubber tyres on a dry road. In the latter case the loss of energy can be sufficient to prevent an accident. A wet surface at similar speed would not support both the grip and wear combined. Some car-makers advertise that their vehicles have "more rubber on the road". The advantage is not to increase friction *per se* but to provide a sufficient area of tyre to transfer the engine power to traction. It is also to increase µ to over 1 by energy absorption in "scrubbing off" a rubber surface[6] whilst maintaining traction. Values of µ for rubber/concrete of over 3 have been recorded.[7] This corresponds to an incredible angle of incline of 71° 34' to move. Bicycle brake blocks are an interesting case in which both high friction and good wearing characteristics are essential. The fact that surface area does not affect friction is demonstrated clearly by the use of small brake blocks and disc brakes. Thus a compromise between ensuring braking power whilst maintaining durability and lightness has to be achieved. Rubber feet on portable workbenches and walking sticks provide high grip. The use of foam rubber bench pads gives grip without marking the workpiece.

A technology which has employed the heat developed by friction is friction welding. A metal rod is pressed against a flat surface and rotated rapidly. The heat developed is sufficient to melt the metals in contact. (This phenomenon is just an extension of the ancient wood fire stick.) The process is also used to join pipes by rotating a collar fitted over the pipe ends.[8]

Although initially wood, and then coal,

powered the industrial revolution, it was drive belts, mainly of leather, which transferred the power to myriad machines. Textiles, toolmaking, rock crushing, and threshing grain are some areas that benefited from the wide flat belts extensively used for 300 years. I recall the traction engines visiting farms to carry out the annual harvest processing. The textile and timber mills had a main drive belt to a line shaft with hundreds of smaller pulleys either in use or waiting to be engaged. The efficiency of transmission of these belts is very high (around 95%) so long as the tension (equivalent to weight for sliding friction) is kept high and the belt surface is kept free of oil. One way of maintaining adhesion between belt and pulley was to paint the pulleys occasionally with a tacky substance, such as honey. Wide belts, as with car tyres, are needed to carry heavy loads at speed. A big industrial belt, made of joined leather sections, could transmit up to 500 H.P (> 350 kw) up to twenty metres. V belt pulleys, of fixed length, tended to replace leather belts when electric motors became common. To get high power transmission, multiple pulleys (or sheaves) would be used in parallel. Recently poly V belts have been introduced. These combine the advantages of a flat belt with the improved lateral stability of V belts on the pulley at high speed (Fig. 4). I have heard people claim that these belts increase the area of contact, hence the friction. This, again, is not the case. Wide poly V belts can transmit equivalent power to a similar cross section of V belts, but they allow very small diameter pulleys to be employed.

Surface roughness
Intuitively one might expect that two flat plates with increasing roughness would provide increased frictional resistance. This is only true in the sense of achieving sufficient force to overcome static friction and cause sliding. Two coarse sandpaper surfaces under load are obviously harder to start sliding against each other than two fine ones. This would show on a graph like Figure 2 as a longer line (same slope) on the static friction region, a larger drop

Fig. 4. Poly V belts allow a compact system of power transmission.

(A_f), but a similar line under identical load for the dynamic region. Experiments over a range of surface roughness values of particular pairs of materials confirm that dynamic friction is independent of roughness.[9] This finding has been explained by pointing out that the energy required to lift a rough surface over bumps is regained on falling down into the valleys. The forward momentum is maintained after the initial motion has been achieved. It is for this reason that if a heavy crate is to be moved by sliding on a concrete floor, it should be done in one continuous motion. Of course, even better, rollers, wheels, or wheels with bearings should be employed. In this context it is of interest of note that wooden rollers were used (albeit rarely) under heavy loads on sledges[10] before 4000 BC. It has been demonstrated recently that the Easter Island statues were transported (1000 to 1500 AD) from their quarries to the coast by similar means.[11] Large boulders in a field obviously do not constitute flat surfaces.

The earliest known wheels (Mesopotamia) are dated just before 3500 BC but they were only used on light carts.[12] Wheels for heavy loads would require good roads; these were not well developed until ancient Persian, Chinese and Roman projects between 500 BC and 150 AD. It is quite impressive that large wheels on light vehicles allow the use of ill defined and inexpensive tracks. On the other hand, well-engineered wheels on rigid tracks produce very low friction. I have seen two men push a small railway engine on to a level turntable. Of course, a slope would be a different matter. Roller bearings of wood and bronze dated at 100 BC were found on a Danish cart.[13] No such device was known to the ancient Chinese, Greek, or Roman world. Leonardo sketched such roller bearings;[14] I am uncertain whether they were used in practice – except in recent models. Modern roller bearings have very low coefficients of friction.

It must be stressed that in surface roughness comparisons, one must compare like with like. A well-kept sole of a metal try-plane cannot be compared with a heavily rusted relative. On the one hand, wood versus iron has a µ value of c. 0.4 whereas wood against iron oxide (rust) has a µ value approaching 0.8.

It will be apparent therefore that the reason hard surfaces such as skis are often highly polished is to reduce static friction. This overcomes any tendency to "bed in" before motion begins (Fig. 2). From the foregoing, it is obvious that the lubrication is the major contributor. However, if two different flat glass surfaces are compared, an interesting result is achieved. Clean ground glass surfaces will glide over each other with ease, whereas if two Pilkington float glass surfaces are placed together, it is almost impossible to slide or pull them apart. This applies also to perfectly cleaved crystal surfaces, e.g. mica. The explanation is very simple; the coarse ground glass surface has sufficient space for a layer of lubricating air between its grooves, whereas the float glass surfaces are in very close and frequent atomic contact. There is an extremely strong attraction between them. A coating of grease between the ground glass surfaces fills the "air space" and actually increases the friction.

Current views

Up until the 1930s it was believed that surface roughness between flat surfaces was the main contributor to friction between two flat objects in contact (Coulomb's theory). This idea, of interlocking causing friction, would predict that increasing roughness would increase friction. Much of the present understanding of metal-metal surface friction has been achieved by the detailed investigation of physicists F.B. Bowden and D. Tabor in Cambridge and Melbourne between 1930 and 1950.[15] Their work has shown that the independence of friction on surface area and roughness is due largely to the fact that in almost all solids there is extremely little actual contact, even on highly polished surfaces. Hence, the pressure on the few points of contact is very high indeed. In dynamic friction the real area of contact is constantly changing. On a microscopic scale, highly polished surfaces exhibit massive peaks and troughs. Secondly, Bowden and Tabor have provided much data to support the theory that friction in "flat" plates is caused largely by atomic attraction at those relatively small number (<1%) of specific points of contact. The fact that increasing the number of point junctions leads to higher friction is illustrated by the float glass observation. For a hard metal sliding on a softer surface, the effect of "ploughing" (scratching) plays a significant part. Coulomb's suggestion of mechanical interlocking by surface roughness is now regarded as having a small effect on smooth metal plates. Of course, on very rough ground a heavy crate or rock is impeded by the terrain and the size of barriers to movement. This is, however, a different phenomenon, one that has been put to effective use for tank barriers.

There are many areas in which Coulomb's theory still holds; in the extreme, teasels and man-made imitations exemplify this. In the textile industry in particular, roughness and smoothness are dominated by the fine structure of the fibres.

Friction and tools

There are many examples where high friction is essential to the efficient working of tools. The inclined plane, whether it be a roof, a plank to a scaffolding, or a vertical screw (e.g. a bottle jack) all rely on a good frictional grip to prevent a load sliding under the force of gravity. Similarly, high friction is necessary for the firm holding of a workpiece in a vice, bench clamp, or a bar/pipe clamp. An interesting, simple device illustrates the two principles of static friction (Fig. 5). Note that whereas the brick paviour on the left is in contact with the majority of the area of the jaw, only a thin line is holding the right hand paviour.

I recall a schoolteacher who would idly form a ream of paper into a helix by rubbing a knuckle round and round the top sheet. The idea was to ease the taking of sheets of paper by examinees. A similar principle is used by a photocopying machine to feed one sheet at a time. The friction drive wheel on a sewing machine and the sheep shearing machine drive, used to transfer power from a wheel and line shaft respectively, employ the same system.

On the other hand, low frictional resistance

Fig. 5. Brick clamp. Same principle employed with quarrymans' shear and handling machines (e.g. the Palfinger) on brick delivery trucks .

is essential to ease the effort required in many manual operations. The driving of a screw or tightening a nut are aided by lubricating oils and soaps. The moving of furniture is eased by low friction pads; more and more machines in the workshop are fitted with wheels or castors which can be engaged or locked. Lifting an extension ladder requires a free fit, and cutting tools such as planes, saws and axes are best operated with the maximum energy devoted to cutting – not being wasted on overcoming friction. That is, they must be sharp.

Plain planes

Although metal-soled planes were made in Britain in the latter part of the 18th century, in the late 19th century makers such as Spiers, Norris, and Mathieson produced heavy planes. They were needed for dense and difficult hardwoods. They were of high quality and price.[16] The somewhat lighter and much less expensive American Bailey-style planes made little headway in Britain until the First World War. Jane and Mark Rees suggest that this was, in large part, due to tradesmen finding that metal planes required more energy in use than their wooden equivalents.[17] This implies that the frictional resistance of the Bailey-style planes was higher than that of wooden ones. The cutting action would, of course, require identical energy with similarly set sharp irons.

As we have seen, the main contributions to friction are weight and the value of μ. Thus an iron plane, twice the weight of a similar sized wooden plane, would require a value of μ half that of wood/wood to display similar resistance. In fact, Bowden and Tabor showed iron/wood and wood/wood values fall within similar ranges.[18] Thus the greater weight is not offset at all by the difference in coefficients of friction. The rationale presented by Rees and Rees is thus supported. By way of demonstration, I compared the frictional forces required to slide equivalent sized iron- and wood-soled planes along various flat surfaces. I used an average of three runs each on radiata (Monterey) pine (*Pinus radiata*) and (Victorian) Mountain ash (*Eucalyptus regnans*). In all cases the wooden plane began to slide under a lower applied load than the heavier iron plane of similar size and duty (Fig. 6). The method used was essentially that of Leonardo, applying weight (dry sand in my case) to a pan hanging from a pulley, carrying a cord to the plane (Fig. 1, method a). The weight of the pan and sand required to be added to cause motion was noted (F). In preliminary trials it was found that the results varied considerably with surface dust and the time between runs. Thus the wood was allowed to cool for five minutes between tests and the surface was vacuum cleaned. The plane surfaces were "dusted" with a fibre (static effect) duster. The main cause of variation was the inertia of a plane resting on the wood before sufficient load was applied (Fig. 2). This was overcome by mounting the boards on a lightly vibrating surface (drill press table).

The results are displayed in Figure 6; in every case, the wooden plane had less frictional resistance than its metal counterpart. It is noteworthy that µ wood/iron and µ wood/beech are 0.34 and 0.37 respectively. Therefore the overriding effect is the greater weight of each metal plane over its wooden counterpart.

Thus the Rees and Rees thesis that a wooden plane requires less effort (Work Done = Force x Distance) than that of a heavier metal plane is confirmed. Garret Hack in his beautiful book preferred to rely on a socio-political explanation.[19] There is a fundamental consequence of the fact that the coefficient of friction wood/beech is slightly higher than that of wood/iron. Attempts to improve metal planes by attaching beech soles are doomed to failure; not only did wooden soles add weight to the metal body, but the surface produced a greater frictional resistance than the one it replaced. Thus from the standpoint of work done by the tradesman, "transition" planes had nothing to offer unless much of the metalwork was replaced by lighter wood.

Friction and corrugated planes

By the mid-19th century the mass production of metal bodied planes was well advanced in North America. Some manufacturers, responding to the finding that heavy iron bodied planes required more effort to use than the traditional wooden planes, sought ways to overcome the problem. The level of engineering skill applied to production was most impressive. However, in light of the foregoing, the degree of analysis of the basis for some of the approaches must be questioned.

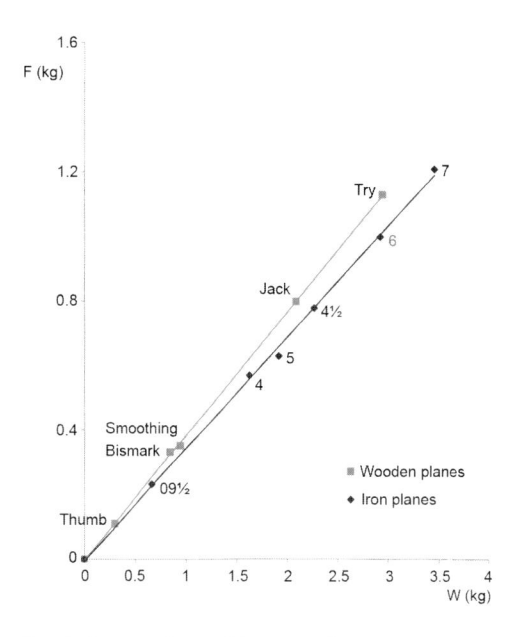

Fig. 6. Comparison of friction of some iron (Stanley /Record numbering system) and wooden planes, cutters lifted.

Examples of the outstanding late 19th century engineering designs devoted to metal sole area reduction are illustrated by Hack.[20] His only support for their use is that they are relatively easy to lap flat, since the metal to be removed is much reduced. A group of beautifully-made small sole-area planes is shown by Sandor Nagyszalanczy.[21] He agrees that none of them helps in friction reduction unless by weight reduction. However, he claims that, "testing by modern physical scientists indicates that machined corrugations, holes, or slots into a plane's sole do not reduce planing friction …" No reference is given, but the foregoing illustrates that this fact has been known to the engineering world for at least a quarter of a millennium.

Tilsby, Race, and Holly Co. produced iron planes for up to ten years following Holly's patent in 1852. No mention of "corrugation" or boring out the sole is made in the specification or the claims (US Patent No. 9,094). Roger Smith reports that the majority of the Holly planes found have machined out (either fluted or drilled) soles (Fig. 7). This, and the fact that

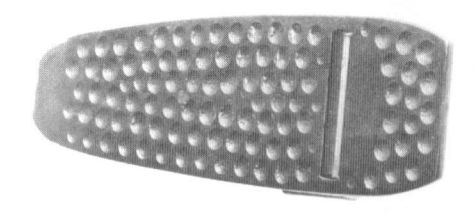

Fig. 7. Two of Birdsill Holly's weight-reduced metal planes.

the soles are tapered from cutter to heel, leads him to suggest that weight reduction was the objective.[22] Weight reduction by metal removal is common in many tools, eg. metal mitre boxes, where good friction is still essential.

Seventeen years after Birdsill Holly's pioneering work in reduction of weight in metal planes, there was a massive flurry of activity in sole area reduction. It has been said that manufacturers were aware of the higher effort required to push metal planes than their wooden equivalents.[23] E.G. Storke appears to have been the first advocate of decreasing contact area to reduce friction "caused by their exact and even faces." Storke was one of many who used "common sense" rather than resorting to the knowledge base. He made the wrong choice, but managed to obtain a patent (US Patent No: 96,052) in 1869 for grooved, fluted, or channelled soles to ease the planing of wood. This pattern persists to this day.

Shortly after Storke, the idea of area-reduction to reduce friction ("in a corresponding ratio") occured to Ellis H. Morris (US Patent No: 109,037 – 1870). The inventor was apparently intent on reducing both weight and friction. Of course, the fact that a flat sole with a ribbed bottom maintained rigidity at a lessened weight allowed him to partially achieve his aim. But the area of contact was not, as he claimed, a contributing factor. Morris' patent bench planes, which were produced by Sandusky, usually have diamond-shaped ridges – ostensibly to avoid the "catching" problems of grooving (Fig. 8).[24] It is, perhaps, equally likely that this was an attempt to avoid the Storke Patent.

C.R. Chaplin (US Patent No: 126,519 – 1872]) ascribed the "increased effort effect" essentially as identical to the increase in atmospheric pressure caused by the "near perfect" sole of metal planes. Use of a microscope of limited power would have discouraged this claim. Chaplin patented the boring of holes in the sole to equalise the pressure above and below the sole. Another, quite ineffective, but beautiful plane is the Rodier patent (Fig. 9). It has wavy "corrugations" cast into the sole, with a view to avoiding "holding up" on corners.[25]

The one iron plane which may well have achieved lowering of friction is the Boston Me-

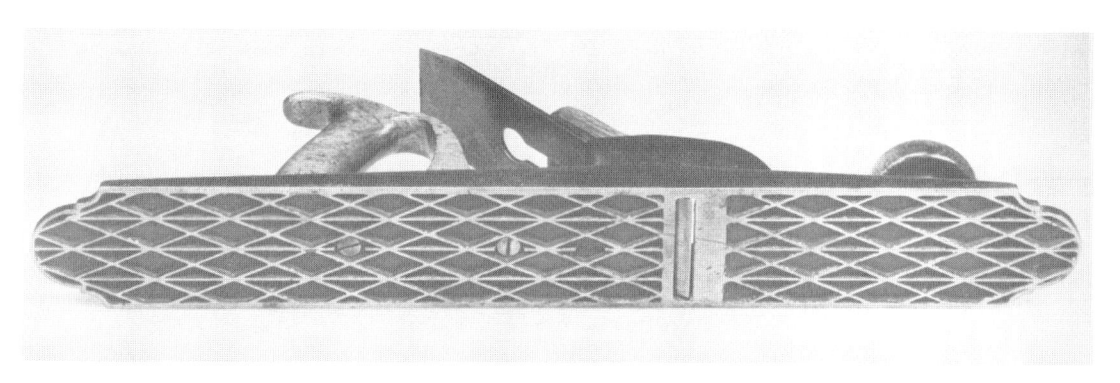

Fig. 8. Morris Patent, weight and area reduction of sole.

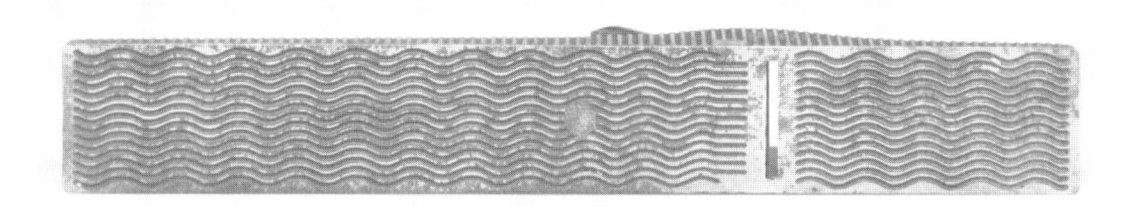

Fig. 9. Rodier's variant on a theme – to avoid catching.

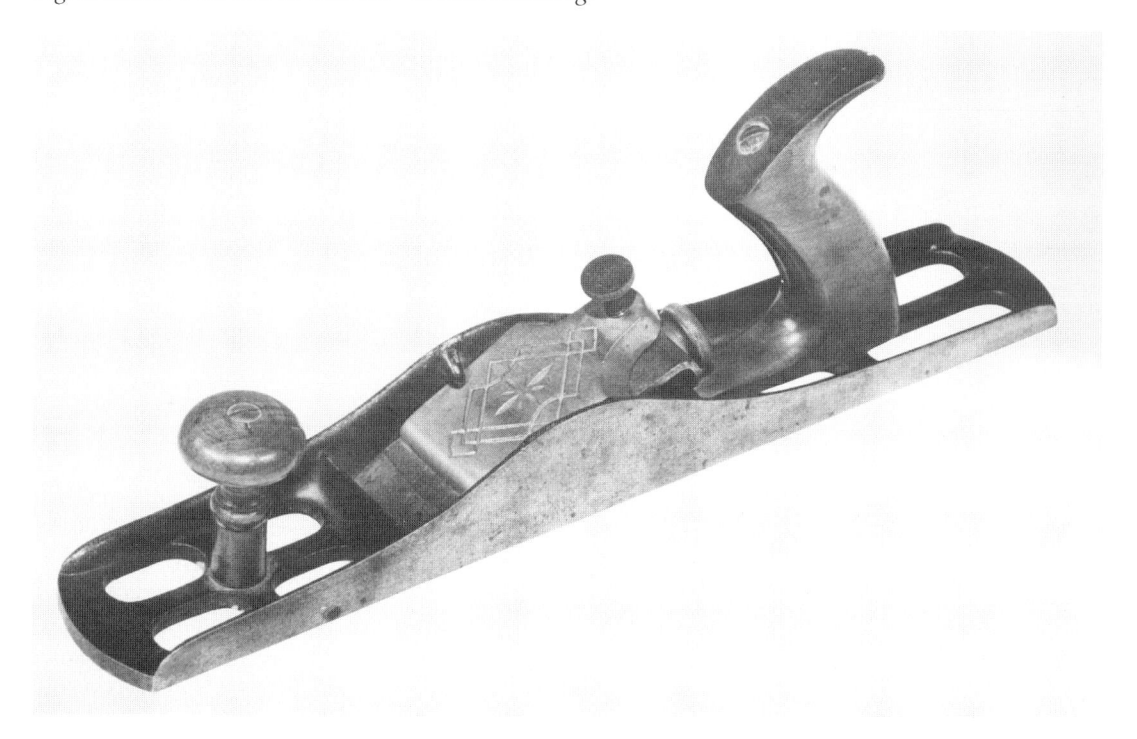

Fig. 10. Boston Metallic Co.'s heavily perforated-sole plane .

tallic model.[26] It has extremely large perforations in the sole which may well reduce the plane's weight to that of an equivalent wooden plane (Fig. 10). This plane seems to have taken Holly's and Chaplin's approaches a big step forward, whether consciously or not.

Four patents were granted to Chaplin between 1888 and 1902 covering fluting to reduce friction and other modifications including cutter adjustment. Chaplin had an impressive range of "corrugated" planes on the market in 1888.[27,28] One design of the Chaplin Patent plane does have a truly corrugated sole; it is the Tower & Lyon plane series nos. 1000 and 1200. The ridges on the top of the sole correspond with the grooves on the bottom (Fig. 11).

In general, the description "corrugated" is rather a misnomer. It normally implies waveforms like corrugated iron and corrugated cardboard. Grooved, fluted, trenched, channelled, or sulcated would serve as more accurate descriptions for this type. However, all manner of surface-reduced planes have been brought under the "corrugated" tag. Area-reduced is a term to cover the gamut of approaches to the style.

In 1890 a very interesting series of Steers' patent planes, by C.E. Jennings & Co., New York, with three rosewood strips inserted in the sole (before and aft of the throat) was launched.[29] The virtue of these lovely planes is stated as "… giving the ease of working of a wood plane, while retaining all the advantages of an iron plane." Evidence for both Chaplin's and Steers' claims was lacking, and as we have seen, replacing an iron surface by a wooden one in a heavy plane can be counter-productive from the point of efficiency. Rosewood may well have a lower μ value than beech, however.

Jacob Siegley was granted a patent (US Patent No: 510,096) in 1893. His early bench planes had grooved soles, not unlike Holly's and Storke's early models. The details of Seigley's initial arrangements with Stanley are not clear. It would appear that Stanley made Seigley planes in a partnership[30] around the turn of the century at about the time they introduced the Stanley C-series of fluted sole planes.[31] I have not found claims by Stanley themselves regarding reduction of friction (as opposed to adhesion). It is my contention that Stanley's engineers would have been quite conversant with the scientific aspects of friction. None the less it would have been desirable to match the product range of competitors. In 1901 J. Seigley advertised a range of fluted iron planes.[32] There is an unequivocal statement "The bottom of the plane, being corrugated … will therefore greatly reduce the friction common to all solid iron bottom planes." This claim and Storke's, Morris', and Chaplin's claims must have been made in ignorance of the (then) 200 years of published work and of any evaluation results on their own products. I find it fascinating that, almost sixty years after Holly's patent, there was so much activity, between 1888 to 1905, in this area. It is also surprising that the efficacy requirement for the granting of patents seems to have been overlooked by the U.S. Patent Office.

Again, experiments were carried out to demonstrate the effect of grooving (Fig. 12). It is clear that the frictional properties of "corrugated" planes do not differ from those of "plain" planes. Both styles fit on the same line; this demonstrates that there is no reduced friction by reducing the surface area of a plane.

Sargent makes a novel passing reference to friction reduction, suggesting some woodworkers prefer planes where "the grooves permit the passing of air and so serve to cool off the heated metal."[33] This appears to display an element of clutching at straws – if not shavings. In later years, manufacturers' claims of friction reduction by machine grooved/drilled (or cast) soles were abandoned. Thus, by the mid-1930s, the suggestion was that the value of the fluted sole lay in holding oil and the avoidance of lifting by suction on thin wide slats[34] and in the handling of particularly resinous South American timbers.[35,36,37] There is no doubt that planing very thin slats can cause

CHAPLIN'S IMPROVED PATENT IRON PLANES
WITH CORRUGATED BOTTOMS
AND CHECKERED RUBBER HANDLES

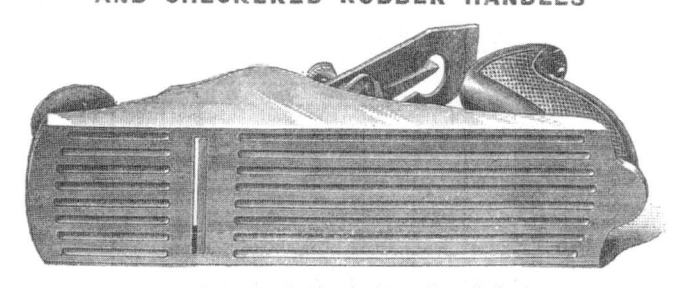

WITH CHECKERED RUBBER HANDLES

No. 1203.	Smooth Plane,	8 in. long—	1¾ in. Cutter	$3 25
" 1205.	"	9 " "	2 " "	3 50
" 1207.	Jack	15 " "	2⅛ " "	4 25
" 1208.	Fore	18 " "	2¼ " "	5 00
" 1210.	Jointer	22 " "	2½ " "	5 75
" 1211.	"	24 " "	2⅝ " "	6 75

With Adjustable Throat

No. 1233.	Smooth Plane,	8 in. long—	1¾ in. Cutter	$3 50
" 1255.	"	9 " "	2 " "	3 75
" 1277.	Jack	15 " "	2⅛ " "	4 50

THE ADJUSTABLE THROAT IS A SUCCESS

WITH WOOD HANDLES

No. 1003.	Smooth Plane,	8 in. long—	1¾ in. Cutter	$3 00
" 1005.	"	9 " "	2 " "	3 25
" 1007.	Jack	15 " "	2⅛ " "	4 00
" 1008.	Fore	18 " "	2¼ " "	4 75
" 1010.	Jointer	22 " "	2½ " "	5 50
" 1011.	"	24 " "	2⅝ " "	6 50

With Adjustable Throat

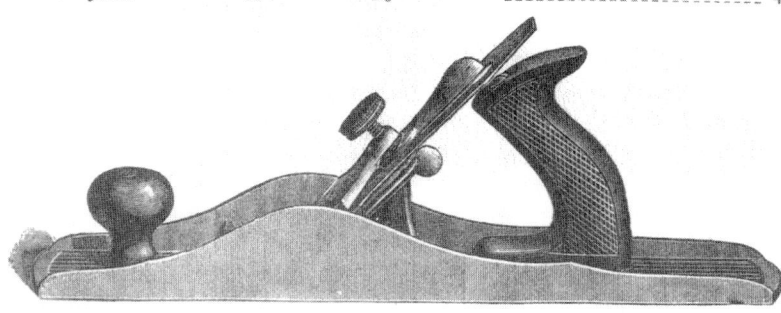

No. 1033.	Smooth Plane,	8 in. long—	1¾ in. Cutter	$3 25
" 1055.	"	9 " "	2 " "	3 50
" 1077.	Jack	15 " "	2⅛ " "	4 25

The **Corrugated Face** has gained the appreciation and approval of the best Mechanics. The ample **air spaces reduce the friction** to a minimum, requiring less effort in use, and by the parallel ribs gaining added strength and rigidity.
The Clamp Plate and Lever are Nickel Plated.

Fig. 11. Tower & Lyon Co. catalogue of c. 1904 showing one of Chaplin's genuine corrugated planes.

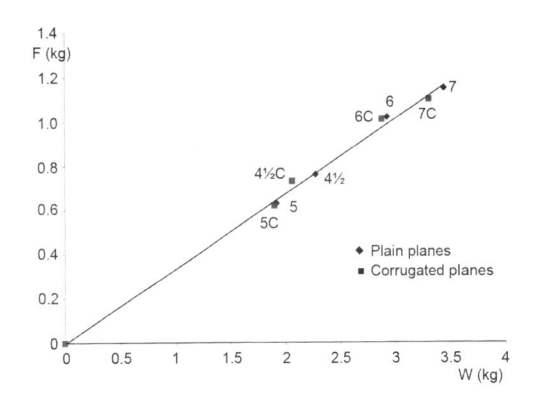

Fig. 12. Friction properties of iron- and "corrugated" iron planes, cutters lifted.

some annoying lifting by temporary suction. The grooves certainly alleviate that problem. Resin adhesion will be reduced by lowering the area of contact. Adhesion and friction both impede motion, but they are entirely different phenomena. Joiners I have spoken to on this subject felt there was no frictional advantage in using these planes. Hack agrees with them.[38] It is, nevertheless, somewhat disturbing to find relatively recent references to reduction of friction by reducing area of contact.[39,40]

Millers Falls made a range of elegant bench planes in the 1950s; they had both conventional and fluted soles. The smoothing plane, 9c, is shown in Figure 13.

Probably the last grooved sole plane to enter production was the Record 735 composite board slitting tool (Fig. 14). A considerable proportion of this plane had the sole surface reduced for no apparent reason. A patent specification covering this plane (A.B. Hampton & M.A. Alexander, GB Patent No: 755,582 –1956) is concerned with achieving optimal angles for setting various blades and attachments for different heads. There is no reference to the provision of grooves in the sole.

Transversely waisted soles
There are two distinct types of transversely relieved-sole planes manufactured. In these tools, part or all the sole is removed ahead of the mouth, and the sole between the mouth and the heel is concave.

A number of Japanese block planes, used to furnish superbly smooth surfaces, have slightly concave sections of sole fore and aft the mouth. Various Western reports suggest this is in part to reduce friction.[41,42] Again the area of contact is not the cause of friction. Friction is the product of force acting perpendicular to the direction of motion and µ for plane/wood. The concavities in the planes will certainly help in easing the tuning of a plane, since the sole requires relatively little material to be removed. A second factor could be that the concentration of force before the mouth compresses the surface slightly. The material would spring back at the mouth opening and allow a very fine shaving to be removed. The safety razor could be seen as a more pronounced example of this phenomenon.

However, the most likely value of using block planes with this design of sole is the quality of finish achieved. Professor W. H. Coaldrake reports that the final smoothing removes continuous shavings of less than 30 microns (0.003mm).[43] The resulting surface is actually water repellent. This could be the result of the high pressure exerted by the lateral ridges of the sole. This pressure probably compresses the exposed cells to give rise to a "burnished" surface. In some softwood timbers the heartwood burnishing might well cause the expression of resinous extractives from the cells. These would cause water repellency.

Stanley offered an interesting roughing plane for a short period (1905 – 1917); it was given the name of a furring plane. This plane has only two areas of contact with the board – at the mouth and the heel. Thus the blade is virtually at the toe of the plane. It could be likened to a spokeshave with a trailing outrigger. Sellens states that the plane provides minimum friction on a rough surface.[44] The manufacturers do not seem to have made that claim; all the foregoing indicates that the suggestion is unfounded, and the plane will

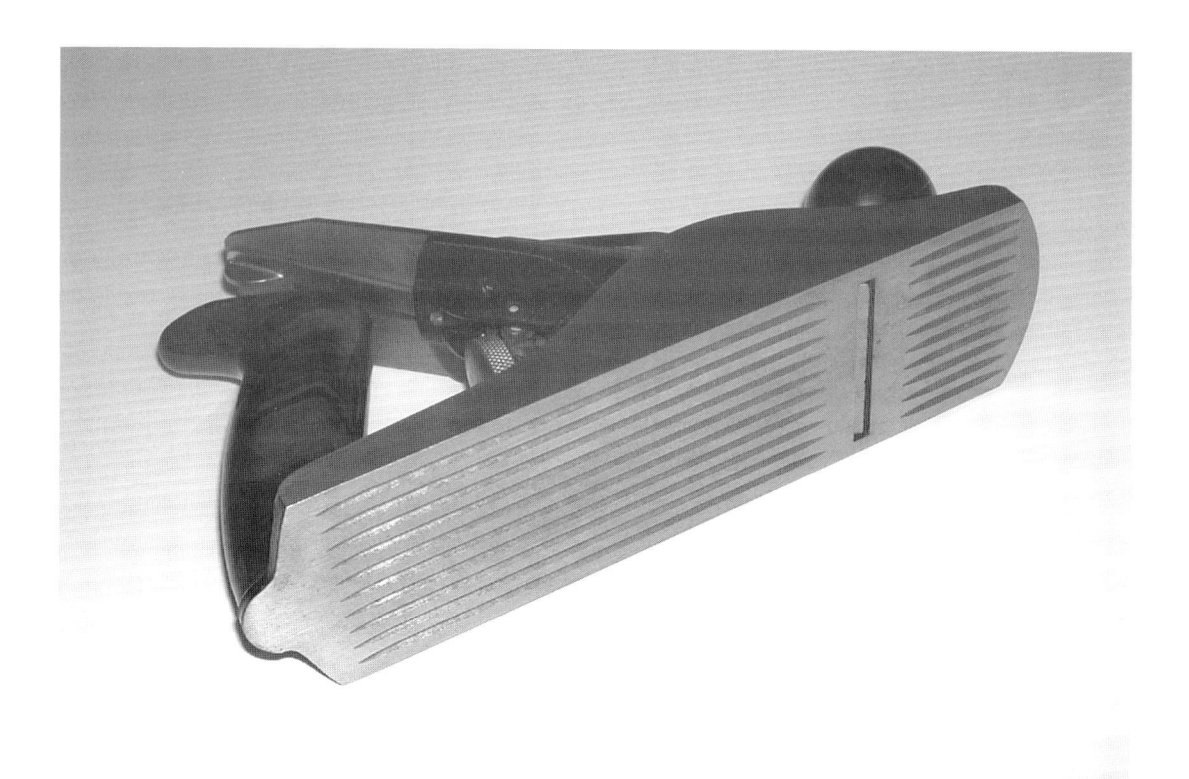

Fig. 13. Millers Falls 9c with fluted sole. The numbering system reflected the length in inches. It was equivalent to other manufacturers' No.4 smoothing planes. (Wal. Maynard's collection).

Fig. 14. Record 735 Slitting Tool. Fitted with hardboard cutting blade to give a 45° mitre. (Author's collection).

simply remove the 'hilltops' whilst following the major undulations of the surface.

Conclusions

Manufacture by Stanley (USA and Australia) of the C series was largely discontinued by the mid-1970s. Until very recently, Stanley still produced four models in Sheffield for world markets.[45] Ostensibly, these planes were aimed at reducing adhesion in working resinous timbers. Record continued production of their fluted planes until sometime between 1993 and 1998, also in Sheffield. The lifespan of the technology was therefore just 150 years; not bad for a feature of limited utility!

Birdsill Holly was a most accomplished engineer in a range of industries. He had over

150 patents.[46] It is more than likely that he knew that reduction in weight, not area, was of utmost importance. All that followed, by way of claims of friction reduction, seems to be just a fad. However, it was a wonderful period for producing some incredible collectors' items. And Japanese block planes with transverse concavities produce beautifully finished surfaces without the need for sanding. But friction reduction is not a contributing factor.

Information on friction research, from the Renaissance period up to the early 20th century, does not appear to have reached entrepreneurial manufacturers of hand planes. Collectors are the richer for a plethora of different designs of sole-reduced planes. Many will have been little used since they confer no friction advantage over their plain-soled relatives, and some have disadvantages.

References

1. F.P. Bowden & D. Tabor, *The Friction & Lubrication of Solids*, Oxford, 1950, pp. 1, 87-89.
2. *Ibid.*
3. D. Dowson, *History of Tribology*, 2nd. ed., London, 1998, pp. 222-231.
4. R.K. Smith, *Patented Transitional & Metallic Planes in America – Vol.II. (PTAMPIA – Vol. II)*, Athol, MA, 1992, pp. 126, 127.
5. McGraw Hill, *Encyclopaedia of Science & Technology*, 9th. ed., 2002, Vol. 7, p. 531.
6. F. Puhn, *Brake Handbook*, Tucson, AZ, 1985, p. 35
7. Dowson, *op. cit.* p. 516.
8. M. Gould, *Principles of Welding Technology*, 2nd. ed., London, 1986, pp. 16-18.
9. Bowden & Tabor, *op. cit.* pp. 87-89.
10. H. Hodges, *Technology in the Ancient World*, New York, 1992, p. 99.
11. J.A. van Tilburg, *Among Stone Giants*, New York, 2003, pp. 241, 242.
12. Hodges, *op. cit.* p. 84.
13. *Ibid.* p. 243.
14. Dowson, *op. cit.* pp. 101-113.
15. Bowden & Tabor, *op. cit.* pp. 87-89.
16. C. Proudfoot & P. Walker, *Woodworking Tools*, Oxford, 1984, pp. 42-62.
17. J. & M. Rees, *Tools – A Guide for Collectors*, 2nd. ed., Needham Market, 1999, p. 144.
18. Bowden & Tabor, *op. cit.* pp. 87-89.
19. G. Hack, *The Handplane Book*, Newtown, CT, 1997, pp. 22, 24.
20. *Ibid.* pp. 43, 44.
21. S. Nagyszalansczy, *The Art of Fine Tools*, Newtown, CT, 1998, p. 145.
22. R.K. Smith, *Patented Transitional & Metallic Planes in America 1827–1927*, 2nd ed. (*PTAMPIA 1827-1927*), Athol, MA, 1990, pp. 38.
23. Rees, *op. cit.* p. 144.
24. Smith, *PTAMPIA 1827-1927,* pp. 112,113.
25. *Ibid.* pp. 183, 184.
26. *Ibid.* p. 152.
27. *Ibid.* p. 163.
28. Tower & Lyon Co. *Catalogue*, c. 1904, reprinted by R.K. Smith, Athol, MA. 1989, pp. 8, 9.
29. Smith, *PTAMPIA – Vol. II*, pp. 142, 143.
30. *Ibid.* p. 333.
31. A. Sellens, *The Stanley Plane*, 1975, p. 35 and numerical listings.
32. Smith, *PTAMPIA – Vol. II*, p. 331.
33. Sargent *Catalogue*, c. 1925, reprinted by R.K. Smith, Athol, MA, 1975, p. 4.
34. C.W. Hampton & E. Clifford, *Planecraft*. Sheffield, (1934), 5th. Impression, 1953, p. 219.
35. Sellens, *op. cit.* p. 35 and numerical listings.
36. Record Tools *Catalogue,* 1963, No. 17, p. 70.
37. Stanley (UK) *Catalogue*, 2001, p. 23, and G. Plaw, personal communication, 2004.
38. Hack, *op. cit.* pp. 43, 44.
39. S. Allen, *Plane Basics*, New York, 1993, p. 14.
40. T. Odate, *Japanese Woodworking Tools*, Newtown, CT, 1984, p. 93.
41. R.S. Newman, "Souping Up the Block Plane", *Fine Woodworking on Planes and Chisels*, Newtown, CT, 1985, pp. 7 – 9.
42. T. Chase, "Japanese Planes", *Fine Woodworking on Planes and Chisels*, Newtown, CT, 1985, pp. 18 – 22.
43. W. H. Coaldrake, *The Way of the Carpenter*, New York, 1990, pp. 66 – 73.

44. A. Sellens, *Dictionary of American Handtools*, Augusta, KS, 1990, p. 338.
45. Stanley (UK), *op. cit.* p. 23.
46. Smith, *PTAMPIA 1827-1927,* p. 38.

Acknowledgements
I am extremely grateful to Ken Turner for his generous efforts in unearthing original product claims for "grooved" planes, and for his comments on an early draft. Kevin Chamberlain's kindness in loaning many of the corrugated planes used to carry out the frictional comparisons is appreciated. I thank Mark Parr of Record, Wal. Maynard, Graeme Plaw, and Ian Stagg, for additional references.

I am indebted to Roger K. Smith for his generosity in allowing the use of the photographs of the majority of the planes illustrated (Figs. 7, 8, 9, 10 & 11) and to Wal. Maynard for the loan of the Millers Falls 9c. I thank Lee Bistrup for the images for Figs. 4, 5, 13 and 14.

I acknowledge the editorial guidance given by Jane Rees and thank her for taking the photographs of Figs. 7 - 11.

Finally, I acknowledge the help of my wife, Rita, in retrieving patent specifications via the internet, and for the preparation of the drafts of this article.

The author
Warren Hewertson is a retired research chemist. He grew up in (now) Cumbria, and obtained his first degree at Nottingham University in 1958. After a short spell in industrial research he completed a Ph.D. at London University in organophosphorus chemistry. He spent two years in Indiana University before taking up a research position in I.C.I. in Cheshire. After twenty years in research, development and management, he accepted a post in Australia as Chief of the Division of Chemical and Wood Technology in CSIRO (The Commonwealth Scientific and Industrial Research Organisation). He is an active member of the Hand Tool Preservation Association of Australia and an interested long distance member of TATHS.

Scythe makers and other metal workers in the parish of Norton, 1533 – 1750

Kathleen M. Battye

In volume 12 of *Tools and Trades*[1] there appeared an article on the metal workers of the north Derbyshire parish of Eckington, using evidence from that parish's probate wills and inventories. The same class which researched the Eckington material then worked on the wills and inventories of Norton, a neighbouring parish, which was once in north Derbyshire, but which is now wholly within the boundaries of the City of Sheffield. In the previous article, using the Eckington evidence, it was suggested that whilst the Eckington metal workers appeared to specialise in the making of sickles, the metal working craftsmen's specialisation in neighbouring Norton was in scythe making. Indeed from work previously done on one particular Norton family it seemed that there could have been in Norton a group of what today would be described as entrepreneurs, who not only made scythes, but who also owned water powered grinding sites and industrial hearths and whose businesses gave employment to other men and families over several generations.

The initial purpose of the research undertaken by the class was to discover whether the probate wills and inventories would show this when the complete body of probate material, 1533–1750, had been transcribed and any evidence contained therein analysed, not just for metal working, but for all social and occupational groupings. As before, the class was directed by its tutor (the author) and was under the auspices of what was then the University of Sheffield's Division of Adult Continuing Education. The original will and inventory documents are held in the Lichfield Record Office (L.R.O.), reference B/C/11 (See Appendix 3 for L.R.O. Pro/Ad no.); they were studied by the class using photocopies made available by Sheffield City Archives (S.C.A.).

The number of wills and inventories studied was 149 between 1533 and 1650 and 149 from 1651 to 1750, giving a total of 298. These were further grouped into occupations, those engaged in metal working, 33 in the earlier period, and 28 in the later one. In the previous Eckington study the metal workers' inventories formed 16.8% of the total occupational grouping, compared to 20.4% in Norton. It also seemed from examining the sum totals

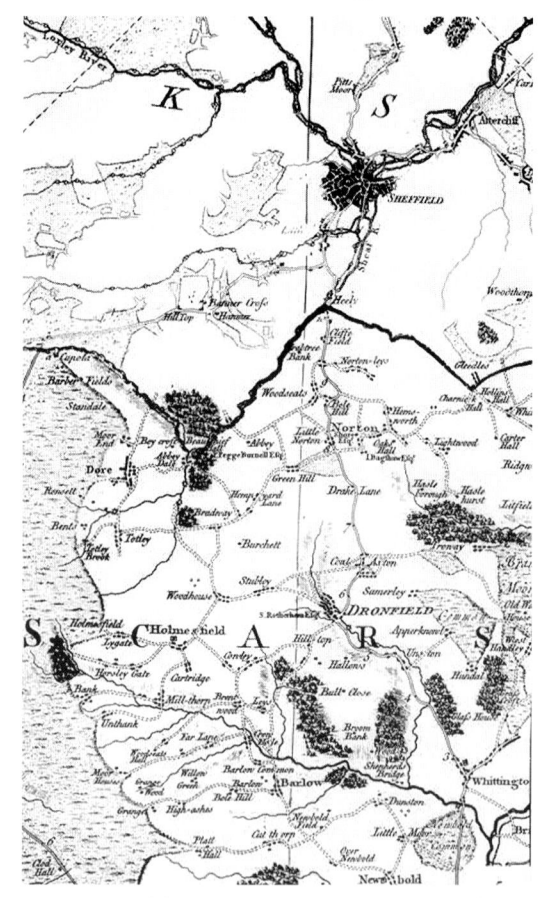

Fig.1. Detail from P. Burdett's 1763-7 map of Derbyshire, 1791 edition. (Norton and its associated hamlets can be seen on the Derbyshire bank of the River Sheaf as it flows on its north-easterly course towards Sheffield.)

of the inventory values over the whole period that the Norton metal workers were more prosperous than those in neighbouring Eckington, 44% of their inventories being valued at more than £75 0s 0d, compared with 32% in Eckington, a significant proportion in both places being valued at more than £100 0s 0d.

As to what size Norton parish was at the time of the study, taking into account the difficulty of obtaining reliable population figures, it would seem that Norton was smaller than its near neighbours, Dronfield and Eckington both in population and in acreage. A Privy Council enquiry into the state of the church in each parish in England and Wales in 1563[2] recorded that the parish of Dronfield had 207 households and that of Eckington, 231, these numbers suggesting population levels of between 931 and 1035 persons for Dronfield and 1039 and 1155 for Eckington, using multipliers of 4.5 and 5.0; their respective areas were given as 6018 acres and 6934 acres. No household number was reported for Norton, but since the parish contained 4630 acres, it may at the time have had a population of around 795. Other population figures from Bishop Compton's census of 1676[3] roughly match the earlier ones, as calculated above, for all three places and confirm that Norton was smaller in both acreage and population than either of its neighbours.

The higher inventory values found in Norton therefore do appear at first sight to confirm the overall importance of the metal working group in that parish and foreshadow the industrial development seen in later centuries.

The 61 metal workers were further divided into different specialisations, either as described in the documents themselves or as they appeared to be from the contents of the inventories or wills. For example, out of the 29 who were involved in the making of scythes, 20 were described as scythe smiths, 4 were yeomen farmers with scythe making implements, materials or made goods in their inventories, 1 belonged to the gentleman class, 1 described himself *"esquire"*, 2 were scythe grinders and 1 was a widow who (as often happened) seemed in her widowhood to have carried on her husband's involvement in the trade. The group designated as smiths appeared from their probate documents certainly to be involved in metal working, but without their particular specialisation being apparent from the inventoried detail. The other widow came into this category. Three men have been included in the list of scythe smiths, although no occupation was mentioned in the documents or, despite the relevant craft items being listed, they were listed as yeomen by their appraisers. When taking his inventory, dated 8 April 1557, Richard Malin's appraisers gave him no occupation but mentioned scythes as

	1533–1650	1651–1750	Total	% of total
Yeomen and husbandmen	54	49	103	34.56
Widows and spinsters	23	22	45	15.10
Gentlemen and clergy	19	16	35	11.74
Non-industrial crafts/trades	17	26	43	14.42
Industrial crafts/trades	2*	0	2	0.67
Metal workers	33**	28***	61	20.46
No occupation assigned	1	8	9	3.02
Total	**149**	**149**	**298**	

*Industrial crafts/trades include 1 charcoal burner and 1 wood collier
**includes 1 sheather (a maker of sheaths for knives)
***2 widows included in metal working total

Table 1: Occupations in wills and inventories for the parish of Norton, 1533 – 1750

	1533–1650	1651–1750	Total
Axe smith	0	1	1
Cutler	3	4	7
Nailer	2	0	2
Sickle smith	0	1	1
Scythe smith	13*	16	29
Sheather	1**	0	1
Smith	14	6	20
Total	**33**	**28**	**61**

* 2 scythe grinders included
** see Table 1 above

Table 2: Metal workers' specialisations in Norton, 1533 – 1750

being owed to him without giving a specific value for them; they also gave 10*d* (10 pence) as the amount owing for what they called *"ale to the watering of scythes"*. In George Urton's inventory of 7 May 1623 a stock of scythes was listed as part of the sum of £80 0s 0d owing to him, although he was described as a yeoman. William Blythe, whose inventory was taken on 7 December 1620, was also described as a yeoman; he was a member of an important scythe making family in Norton; his appraisers listed £58 2s 4d worth of craft items in his smithies without giving any details. Two of his descendants later in the 17th century had prospered greatly and had large quantities of made scythes in their inventories, amounts owing to them also being listed as due for scythes already supplied or in transit. No blacksmiths' inventories were found either in the metal working category or in the group of non-industrial crafts and trades.

Probate material such as wills and inventories, however fascinating and intriguing it may be in showing the detail of men's and women's lives and dwelling places, has its limitations. Wills may show the testator's wishes in the disposition of property and money; they may reveal something about the testator's family, although not all family members are necessarily mentioned; they may also refer to land leased or otherwise held in different parishes or they may give no detail at all; and they may or may not say anything about the testator's occupation and the tools of his or her trade. Inventories can be similarly inconsistent. Appraisers had no given standard to use when listing the deceased's goods and chattells. Some appraisers, who could be local men often in the same trade as the deceased, listed and valued everything in minutely satisfying detail, mentioning buildings, crops, livestock, husbandry gear, rooms in the house and household goods, as well as the deceased's debts and money owing to him or her. In other inventories the detail given is sparse or else groups of possessions are lumped together and given an overall value. Often this was because the deceased was no longer in productive work due to age or infirmity. At other times it could possibly be concluded that the appraisers were careless or even incompetent. Any study of probate material has to accept these limitations, expanding poorly delineated detail from other sources possibly just as imperfect. Reaching firm conclusions from such sources is always suspect. Working empirically, all that can be done is to base conclusion or theory on the information given and try to confirm it using other sources.

Wheels and wheel sites

Metal workers of whatever kind needed access to water powered mill sites for grinding the blades they were making. As regards the Norton craftsmen these sites were mostly on the river Sheaf, which at the time under consideration was the boundary between Yorkshire and Derbyshire, the Norton mills being on the Derbyshire bank. Two of Norton's enterprising scythe makers leased wheel sites on another of the Sheffield area's rivers, the Loxley, a few miles north of the Yorkshire/Derbyshire county border; these sites will be identified in the discussion of the information contained in the documents.

The fifteen references to wheels in the documents are made in different ways. The place names and references given in the documents themselves can indicate the presence of grinding wheels. Cliff Field and Cliff Field Yate were situated in a district now more usually called Woodseats, just above the valley of the River Sheaf and were associated with several scythe making families, Goddards, Brownells and Barnes. On his marriage in October 1604 John Barnes is recorded in the parish registers as being of Cliffield Wheel, but in his will 36 years later he gave his place of residence as Garlick Wheel, a name interchangeable with that of Cliffield Wheel; his widow, Dorothy, married William Vessey and when she died in 1664 she also was described as being of Garlick Wheel. After her marriage this same wheel was referred to in parish registers as Vessey Wheel, this still being used as a place name until 1704.[4] Another named wheel reference occurs in the inventory of William Blythe's goods in February 1632 when the lease of Heeley mill and wheel is valued at £6 13s 4d. (It is usual in the north Derbyshire and Sheffield area to describe the whole area where a grinding wheel with its associated buildings was situated as "wheel" or, for example, "scythe-wheel", so this meaning will be assumed in any examples given.)

Much more frequent are the references to the men and families who occupied the wheel sites for their metal working activities, although this makes the identification of a particular wheel site more difficult, since sites may have changed hands several times over the period of this study. The example given above showing how the same wheel was referred to in different ways over a hundred year period illustrates the point.

An early instance of this is in another John Barnes' inventory of February 1603 when among the debts owing to him were scythes at Robert Barnes' wheel; a Robert Barnes, who may have been John Barnes' father, himself died in March 1603, the entry in the parish register[5] identifying him as a scythe grinder of Cliffield Wheel. There are references in parish registers and other documents to this prolific scythe making family in Norton over many generations and another reference to them is in 1616 in the will of John Parker of Lees Hall, Norton Lees, esquire. He bequeathed to his widow, among other land and leases, the water wheels occupied by Richard Cowley and the scythe wheel occupied by William Barnes. Richard Cowley was a cutler who died in 1624; the Cowleys seem also to have been associated with corn mill sites in Bradway, part of Norton parish; they can also be found among the metal workers in the Renishaw district of neighbouring Eckington parish.[6] William Barnes was, of course, yet another member of the same scythe making family previously mentioned. The wheel in question may be the one referred to as New Mill in a lease granted to John Parker in 1582 and sold by his brother, Francis, to John Bullock in 1622.[7]

Another family name occurs in Thomas Bower's inventory in 1640 in which nine dozen scythes are valued at £9 0s 0d at what the appraisers called John Gillot's wheel. Bower's inventory value was not high at £33 3s 4d, so it could be that he perhaps was renting time on Gillot's wheel.

Appraisers sometimes, of course, merely listed "gear at the wheel" or "wheel gear", or, when listing made goods, "scythes at the wheel", in so doing confirming that the deceased person had rented a wheel, or part of a wheel, but without giving any indication as to its situation. Family connections with a particular part of the Norton bank of the River Sheaf, however, do provide clues as to which wheel site is involved. For instance, the inventories of Edward Brownell in 1686 and Hugh Goddard in 1695 mention scythes at the wheel and both men were also described as being of Cliffield.

Tools at the wheels are mentioned in only seven of the documents. Among these, Richard Cowley, cutler, in his will of 14 February 1625 bequeathed his bellows, stithy and all tools belonging to his smithy, together with the wheel stones, axletrees and wheel gear to Hugh Cowley's son, Robert, who may have been his nephew. George Hobson has been designated a smith, for the want of any specific detail, but may have been a cutler, since his inventory lists three glasiers (a glazing i.e. polishing, tool – this and other specialist terms are explained in the glossary) and a vice among his craftsman's tools; his wheel gear bands, axletree and pulley were valued at 6s 0d. The appraisers of scythe smith Thomas Wainwright's inventory of 1680 merely mention "wheel things" and value them at 5s 0d, whilst John Gillot, scythe smith's, wheel tools were valued at £1 10s 0d in his inventory of 1691. Richard Gillot died in September 1691 and among the craftsman's equipment listed at his wheel were grinding tools and scythes valued at £2 10s 0d and a grinding stone valued at £8 0s 0d.

The will of Robert Barnes of Cliffield Wheel, who died in March 1603, was proved in the Prerogative Court of Canterbury on 20 February 1607 (Prob. 11/109 PRO). In it he bequeaths his tools at the wheel to his eldest son, John: "… *one little temperinge Stedie or Anvile, one little paire of bellowes w(i)thin my wheel house heare, and all the residue of my temperinge geare or implements …one hatchett, one hande sawe, one hammer, one pike, and one thissell. And all my terme, use and interest which I have to come in two Iron axxletrees, and two paire of trindles…*". (See glossary in Appendix 2 for explanation of terms.)

Grindstones

Robert Gillot was a scythe grinder who died in March 1628; his appraisers did not value his craftsman's equipment very highly, valuing his three axletrees, bellows and stithy at 10 s 0d, but thought it worth recording that he had two loads of what they called "*Grennawe stones*" at the wheel, as well as another load still at "*Grennawe*", their total value being put at £1 15s 0d. Loads of stone were also listed in the previously mentioned inventory of Thomas Wainwright. In common with several other metal workers, he was of Cliff Field Yate and seems to have had two smithies, workshops and an iron house there. The total value of his craftsman's equipment came to £48 15s 4d and included £8 15s 0d for seven loads of stone and £1 16s 0d for four loads of rough stone.

George Turner, scythe smith, was in what appears to have been a different league from most of the other metal workers. His total inventory value came to £861 6s 6d in 1716 and his craftsman's equipment totalled £225 8s 0d. He may have owned, or been renting, a wheel at Loxley, since he had a stock of made scythes there worth £106 10s 0d. Not only that, the appraisers mention separately grindstones from Bole Hill at the Loxley wheel to which they gave a value of £9 0s 0d and Wharncliff[e] stone and other stone worth £2 0s 0d.

Bole Hill is a fairly common place name in the north Derbyshire/south Yorkshire area, associated with hilltop wind assisted lead and iron smelting sites and there is a part of Norton parish with that name on the slopes above the valley of the river Sheaf. Whether grindstones were quarried there is not known to the author. There certainly were quarries of the local coal measure sandstone suitable for grinding in both Grenoside and Wharncliffe. Wharncliffe, in south Yorkshire a few miles north of Sheffield, is a place where references to good quality stone used for the grinding of blades occur in the 16th century or earlier.[8] It is also not far from the river Loxley where George Turner had his wheel. The "*Grennawe*" referred to in Robert Gillot's inventory is probably Grenoside, a place name meaning "quarry hill" and which lies within the district of Sheffield known historically as Hallamshire.[9] Wharncliffe Crags and Grenoside are a few miles from one another on the high ground east of the valley of the river Don, upstream of its confluence with the Loxley.

Robert Barnes, scythegrinder, of Cliffield

Fig. 2. An engraving showing scythe grinders at work. (From Sheffield City Libraries Local Studies Leaflet on the Watermills of Abbeydale, Rosamund Meredith.)

Wheel has already been mentioned.[10] Amongst his craft items was another bequest to his eldest son, John, of a load of Ashdon "grindlestones", three Ulley stones and one Ayame stone. Ulley lies in what is now known as South Yorkshire, a short distance approximately due east of Sheffield; Ashdon may refer to Aston, also east of Sheffield, and Ayame is a possible reference to Eyam in the Derbyshire Peak District.

Out of the 61 metal workers' probate documents, thirteen refer to the stones used to grind the blades. The most significant of these have already been mentioned. Some other inventories include such stones amongst other equipment and give them a value, although the same difficulty arises with the valuations as before, some stones being recorded with other items of equipment, making it impossible to compare one reference with another.

Scythe smith John Boer in 1567 had a glasier and a grindstone, valued together at 10s 0d. The list of equipment in John Barnes' smithy when his inventory was taken on 4 February 1603 included a grindstone, two rakes and a "harthstaff" valued at 2s 0d out of a total for his smithy gear of £6 4s 10d. Edward Hudson in 1622 had *"certayne wall stone and one grindeinge stone w(i)th the axeltree...vis viiid"*. William Blythe's appraisers in February 1632 made a very detailed inventory of his goods which included the contents of two mills, a wheel and two smithies. At the corn mill in East Hall meadow among other things were a pair of millstones with rind and spindles valued at £5 0s 0d; at the Heeley wheel were an axletree, a pair of spindles, a trough, a little stithy, a pair of bellows, two pairs of tongs and six loads of stone, valued all together at £5 0s 0d. William Blythe's son, another William, in 1666 had two pairs of stones valued at £5 0s 0d, as well as fourteen new stones and 25 worn stones valued at only £4 0s 0d. James Atkin's craftsman's gear in 1683 included *"three grindell stone axelltrees and one whitin stone …6s 8d"*. Hugh Goddard in 1695 had a cool trough and a grindstone in his upper smithy worth 9s 6d and another cool trough and grindstone in the nether smithy worth 6s 6d.

The other inventories where grindstones are mentioned refer to loads of stone rather than individual stones. Robert Gillot's three loads of *"Grennawe"* stone in 1628 valued in total at £1 15s 0d were worth 11s 8d per load. Thomas Wainwright's seven loads of stone at his wheel in 1680 were worth £1 5s 0d each and the four loads of rough stone 9s 0d each. In 1716 George Turner's grinding stones from Bolehill at his Loxley wheel were worth £9 0s 0d and the stones from Wharncliff £2 0s 0d, but the appraisers do not make it clear how many of the stones were at the Loxley wheel or whether Bolehill stones were deemed more valuable than those from Wharncliff. Possibly the rough stone such as is found in Thomas Wainwright's inventory was un-worked. Without evidence, so far lacking, from other inventories or from the quarry sites themselves, there seems no way of comparing the value of a load of e.g. *"Grennawe"* stone in 1628 with that of either Wharncliff or Bolehill stone in 1716. It is even difficult to speculate at all as to why stone from these named places is distinguished from other loads of unidentified stone and from the single grinding stones in use in the smithy or at the wheel. The conclusion perhaps is that the named stones were known to be especially good and were bought and used by those who could afford to do so.

Smithy hearths

The possessing or leasing of a grinding wheel was obviously important in the Norton metal workers' working lives, even although there are relatively few precise references to either circumstance in the inventories. References to that other important structure, the smithy, are more frequent, but even here the appraisers did not always record its existence clearly. Evidence from the inventories seems to indicate that the smithy formed part of the layout of the buildings on the site where the scythe smiths, cutlers or other smiths lived and worked. In most cases the appraisers listed farming items, including animals and crops, sometimes along with the contents of a barn, suggesting that the smithy formed part of the complex of farm buildings. If the smithy was one of the group of structures on the grinding wheel site, that is never made clear in the documents.

In the 61 metal workers' documents there are 47 possible references to smithies. In 21 of these one smithy is mentioned and there were nine references to smithy gear; one man had an axehouse, four men are listed as having shops or workshops, one man seems to have had more than one smithy, the precise number not being given, five men had two smithies, one of them being William Goddard. He described himself as a yeoman in his will of 1 April 1702 in which he bequeathed smithy gear for two smithies to his brother Thomas when he was 21. Two men had more than two smithies and one man had three. There was one man with an iron house as well as a smithy, one with two smithies and an iron house and one with an iron house and three workshops.

In fourteen documents no smithy or workshop is mentioned; in five of these, no craft gear of any kind is listed; in others only such basic tools as bellows, hammers and stithy are mentioned, suggesting that the deceased's working life was over perhaps due to illness or advancing years. This impression is confirmed in one or two cases similar to that of Thomas Came of Greenhill whose inventory was taken on 28 January 1603. Only an old stithy, a landiron, half an unburned bloom of iron, two dozen old scythes and two old sallets, are recorded, valued altogether at £2 11s 4d out of a total value of £19 6s 4d. He was only in his early thirties when he died and may have been ill and unable to work, which would account for the low value placed on his craft goods, the unused iron and the description of the made scythes and sallets as "old". If he had a smithy at the time of his death, it was out of commission.

Thomas Warter's inventory was taken on 1 June 1683. He had £30 0s 0d out on security credited to him, as well as £3 6s 8d referred to as a desperate debt out of a total inventory value of only £35 2s 7d. His appraisers called him a scythe smith, but listed neither smithy nor craft items among his goods; he appears to have been a bachelor. His executrix was his mother, Elizabeth, to whom he left the residue of his small estate "… *for consideration of her care and Charges of me in all my time of sickness…*" after paying legacies to his brother and his nephew. His nephew's legacy of £5 0s 0d was to be raised from the sale of Thomas Warter's household goods and was "… *to be paid to his Master whom he shall choose to teach him a trade upon the sealing of his Indentures …*". The total value of the estates of these two men was low and their possessions few.

The inventory of George Urton alias Steven presents a different picture, although the same conclusion about the reason for his lack of tools can be drawn. The inventory was taken on 7 May 1623 and in it no tools or equipment relating to his trade are mentioned. George was thirty-six years old when he died and had two young children, a daughter aged three and a son of one year. He was one of a family of yeomen at Lightwood in Norton, all involved in metal working, whose inventories range in date from 1572 – 1630. The earliest of these, Richard Urton alias Steven, was described in his inventory of 12 August 1572 as a scythe smith. He had a smithy, the total value of all his goods being £152 7s 4d; out of this, his smithy gear was £7 0s 0d and his craft goods £122 12s 0d. This latter sum included 1200 scythes at £8 0s 0d per 100 and 12 packs of sickles at £2 4s 4d per pack.

Richard seems to have died childless, an entry in the parish registers recording the burial of triplets in 1565 with no further baptisms recorded.

Richard's brother, Henry, also of Lightwood, died in September 1591 with goods valued at £124 1s 2d, roughly 50% of this value being derived from his farming. Nevertheless, the buildings included a smithy, which had been bought from Anthony Babington of Dethick and which was occupied by John Barnes; in it were three anvils, two pairs of bellows and smithy gear given a value of £4 6s 0d. This smithy was bequeathed to his son, Francis, then aged 14, and smithy gear for one hearth to his son, James, then aged 23. Henry was described as a yeoman of Lightwood, but had obviously carried on the family's involvement in metal working.

John, another brother of Richard Urton alias Steven, also of Lightwood died in 1593. He too was described as a yeoman with nearly 60% of the value of his goods derived from farming, but must have carried on the family involvement with scythe making. He left to his

This Inventory indented made the xiith Day of August anno Domini 1572 specyfyethe the gudds and catelles of Rychard Urton alias Steven at the Day of his deathe ....

Item all the smethe geyre		*vii li*
Item xii hundrethe sythes every hundrethe viii Li	*iiii^{xx}*	*xvi li*
Item xii packs of syckylles ev(er)y price		
after xliiii s iiii d the packe		*xxxvi li xii s*

Extract from inventory of Richard Urton alias Steven, 13th August 1572 (LRO 1574-04-20). Note: li = £ from the Latin form.

> *Item ii stithies*   liii s   iiii d
> *Item ii paire of bellowes with all other Smithie*
>   *gear belonginge to one herthe*   xxvii s   viiid

Extract from inventory of John Urton alias Steven, 12th January 1593 (LRO 1593-06-21).

> *In the Shop*
> *two pair of Bellows three Steddes hamers and tongs two saws*
> *two pair of Vise Other goods belonging to trade as Eight stones*
> *for grinding Pullies and Axeltrees*   £11 15s 0d

Extract from the inventory of Wm. Atkin, 12th October 1710 (LRO 1710-11-14).

great nephew, Edward Urton alias Steven, £10 in money, one stithy, one pair of bellows and all the smithy gear belonging to one hearth when he came of age at 21 if he was willing to be an apprentice *"to use and handle the said Smithie gear in the Science Arte …(as)… the same are to be used or occupied …"*.

His inventory, shown at the top of this page, lists the contents of another house of his in a part of Norton called the Herdings.

All the Urton alias Steven family were probably scythe smiths, as was George, since iron, steel and scythes in his stock were included in the undetailed total of £80 0s 0d owing to him when he died in 1623, this sum forming the major part of the value of the estate of £93 17s 8d, which he left to his wife. No craft gear of any kind and no smithy were recorded by his appraisers.

William Atkin was the only sickle smith found in this study. His inventory, taken on 12 October 1710, refers to a shop rather than a smithy, the three appraisers listing its contents as shown above.

William Atkin had a widow and eight children surviving him when he died aged 74; he left what in his will he called his *"shopp goods and tooles belonging to the Trade"* equally between his eldest sons Samuel, aged 30, and William, who was 29. There are no made goods, nor is there a stock of iron and steel in the inventory, so, judging from the list of basic equipment in the workshop it seems probable that these two sons had taken over their father's business already. William Atkin had had a full working life, for it is probably his name which appears with those of 25 other men in the hearth tax of 1672 listing those smiths who refused to pay this tax levied not just on their domestic, but also on their industrial hearths. His will suggests that William Atkin was fully in possession of his wits, although *"aged and weake of body"*. The inventory with its total value of £119 6s 6d, including a sum of £58 0s 0d for his farming goods, seems to indicate a dual occupation on what could well have been an inherited yeoman holding.

Men such as those mentioned above may either have been at the end of their working lives, or too ill to work, but the hearth tax of 1672 gives a useful list of those 26 smiths in Norton parish who were operating at that time and who were disputing the levying of that tax on industrial hearths. As was the case with William Atkin, it is possible to connect some of the names on the 1672 list with those of men contained in the probate documents, some directly, such as Atkin, who would then have been 36 years old, others because of their family name and connections. The 26 men of 1672 had between them 35 hearths. Those with one hearth numbered 19, five men had two hearths and two men had three.

Of the 26 men on the hearth tax list, the names of eleven appear also in the list of metalworkers' probate documents, either because of a family link before 1672 or because they or their descendants feature on the list.

Name	No. of hearths	Occupation*	W & I
Bartram, William	1		
Gillott, Joseph	1	Scythe smith	(1712 Joshua G. scythe smith)
Goddard, Hugh	2	Scythe smith	1695 H. Goddard
Barton, William	1		
Anderton, George	1		(1630 John A. sheather)
Gillott, R.	1		(1628 Robert G. scythe smith)
Clay, Robert	1		
Atkins, William	2	Sickle smith	1710 Wm. Atkin
Biggin, Thomas	1		(1728 Sam. B. scythe smith)
Jackson, Joseph	1	Cutler	1709 Jo. Jackson
Beckin, William jnr.	1		
Bates, James	1	Cutler	
Biggin, James	3		(1750 Ezra B. scythe smith)
Beckin, William snr.	1		
Gillott, Richard	2	Scythe smith	1691 R. Gillott
Atkins, Frances	1		
Holland, Robert	1		(1614 Robert H. scythe smith)
Barton, Joseph	1		
Brownell, George	2		
Brownell, Edward	1	Scythe smith	1686 Ed. Brownell
Gillott, Richard	1		
Roper, Thomas	1		
Spencer, Thomas	1		
Turner, George	2	Scythe smith	1716 Geo. Turner
Wainwright, Robert	2	Scythe smith	1701 R. Wainwright
Wainwright, Thomas	3	Scythe smith	1680 T. Wainwright

* *Occupations as found in parish registers and probate inventories and wills. Those in brackets refer to men with a family connection to those in the 1672 list.*

Table 3: Norton Smithy Hearths in the 1672 Hearth Tax [11]

Not all the men on this list were scythe smiths, although the majority certainly were. William Atkin, as has been pointed out, was a sickle smith, the Anderton family is referred to as sheathers in 1630, and Joseph Jackson, James Bates and the Barton family were cutlers.

Most of the names can be found in the parish registers, many dating back three or four generations. The Norton baptism registers often give the father's occupation, which is an aid to identification when there are several men in one family with the same forename. Because of this, it is possible to see that the same occupation e.g. that of scythe smith not only applied through the generations, being handed down from father to son, but also that three or sometimes four brothers were engaged in the trade.

The name Gillot (with variations in spelling) appears very frequently in Norton parish registers, many of them in the hamlets of Bolehill and (Norton) Lees, all of them in the scythe making trade. Four men in this family are named in 1672. Joseph Gillot had one smithy hearth in 1672 as did Joshua Gillot when he died in 1712. The inventory value of his bellows, stithy, tempering bellows and all the tools belonging to his smithy was £4 10*s* 0*d*. Robert Gillot, who died in 1628, has already been mentioned. His son, Robert, was born in 1611 and he it is who is probably mentioned as having one hearth in 1672, the list merely referring to R. Gillot. There were two

Richard Gillots in 1672, one with two hearths and the other with one. Richard Gillot of Bolehill's inventory was taken on 9 September 1691 and records the contents of two hearths at what were called the far smithy and the near smithy where his tools were valued at £4 0s 0d, his smithy gear at £4 0s 0d, his tempering tools at 8s 0d and his stock of made scythes at £16 0s 0d. The iron in his iron house was worth £14 3s 6d, a grinding stone at the wheel £8 0s 0d and other tools and scythes there £2 10s 0d; coals, possibly charcoal, were worth a further £3 5s 0d and the value of all his craftsman's gear a total of £53 4s 6d. Richard Gillot was owed over £80 0s 0d and had £160 0s 0d worth of silver in his chest, making an overall total of £407 18s 6d, a considerable sum in 1691.

All the references to the many members of the Goddard family in the parish registers designate them as scythe smiths. Hugh Goddard, who appears in the 1672 list, lived in a part of Norton parish called Trouthouse. His inventory was taken on 27 June 1695 when he would have been 61 years old. It shows him to have been prosperous, the sum total of his goods coming to £276 18s 5d. He was taxed for two hearths on the 1672 list, the detail in his inventory bearing this out. He not only had an upper and a nether smithy, but also an iron house. Although not one of those mentioned in 1672, Hugh Goddard's brother, William, was also a scythe smith. In his will of 1702 he bequeathed his smithy to his nephew, Hugh, thus continuing the family connection with the scythe making trade. Hugh Goddard's son, Thomas, took out a 21 year lease in 1740 on what came to be known as the Abbeydale Works on the River Sheaf in another part of Norton parish and with other enterprising men developed the site, their efforts continuing up to 1802, after which the works were further developed by other tenants. [12]

The Robert Holland listed in 1672 is probably the nephew mentioned in the will of Robert Holland in 1614; he is described as a scythe smith, as is the elder Robert, and received the rest and residue of his uncle's estate, although its inventoried contents suggest that there was little for him to inherit.

The Brownells were a very prolific family, there being five men of that surname, George, Robert, Henry, Jerome and William, all of them scythe smiths and all with children listed in the parish registers from 1563 onwards. They may have been brothers; they were certainly related. Three of these men or their descendants married into other scythe makers' families; George Brownell married Anna Holland in 1596, Henry Brownell married Sara Gillot and William married Helen Gillot. The two Brownells in the 1672 list, George and Edward, may have been brothers or possibly cousins; Edward's baptism is not recorded in the Norton parish registers and until the baptism of his first child in 1668 Edward is not a forename which is used in the Brownell family.

George Brownell was the grandson of Henry, who died in August 1634, eight months after the death of his own son, George. This latter George bequeathed a stithy to each of his sons, George and Leonard and they received

Fig. 3. The scythe workshops at Abbeydale ceased operations in 1935. The site, now known as the Abbeydale Industrial Hamlet is open to the public. (Photograph Lynsey Nuttall)

In the Upper Smythy
One Stythy and one pair of Bellowes and the Hamer and tonges in
And belonging to the Smithy Strings and Sythes vizt
3 dozen of Strings and Four Sythes and two hundred of iron — 06li 3s 4d
In the Nether Smythy
One Stithy and one pair of Bellowes and the Hamers and tonges
In and belonging to the Smithy — 03li 13s 8d
Two Packes of Steele — 04li 16s 0d
One Cart and a wheele barrowe — 00li 14s 0d

Extract from inventory of Ed. Brownell, 20th March 1686 (LRO 1686-04-21).

from their grandfather in his turn all his smithy gear and tools between them when he died. Henry Brownell leased land at Maugherhay in Norton and the wording of the will suggests that his smithy was here, although his four roomed house was at nearby Jordanthorpe. His inventory value totalled £132 3s 6d including the money owed to him. Among his goods were 200, 4 dozen and 8 scythes valued at £17 5s 4d. Thirteen men owed him £62 14s 10d, his own debts to nine men amounting to £20 17s 10d.

Edward Brownell died in 1686. Both his inventory and his will describe him as a scythe smith of Cliffield. He may have been in his mid forties when he died. The terms of his will certainly suggest that he had a young family, everything being left to his wife, Elizabeth, to bring up and educate their six surviving children. The youngest were Ann, aged two years and his only son Edward, aged four, the eldest Elizabeth, aged eighteen. Edward Brownell is taxed for only one hearth in 1672, but his inventory taken fourteen years later on 20 March 1686 lists two smithies and their contents (see above).

George Turner was taxed on two smithies in the 1672 list and so it appears from his inventory, Isaac Bingham and John Gillot being named as working in them. As mentioned above in the discussion regarding wheel sites and the materials found there, George Turner was very prosperous, owning land in Hooton Pagnell, east of Barnsley in the former West Riding of Yorkshire, as well as in Norton and Sheffield. His appraisers valued the iron and steel in both smithies at £1 10s 0d, together with an axletree worth 10s 0d. As mentioned previously, George Turner had a stock of finished scythes at Loxley, valued at £102 0s 0d, six dozen scythes in the same place worth £4 10s 0d and scythes in the smithy occupied by Isaac Bingham and Joseph Gillot worth £2 5s 0d, making a grand total for his made goods of £108 15s 0d. He was owed yet another total sum of £103 13s 0d for made scythes, the appraisers referring to what they describe as *"a Book of Particulars under the Testators Hand"*; his craftsman's equipment, including unsold scythes and those sold but still owed for, iron and steel and grinding stones, totalled £225 8s 0d.

Wainwright is the name of another family in Norton whose connections with the making of scythes can be traced back several generations with the aid of the parish registers. The two Wainwrights listed in 1672 were Thomas, who died in October 1680 and his brother Robert, who died some twenty years later. Thomas was taxed for three smithies, which appear as *"shops"* in his inventory of 16th October.

Robert Wainwright was taxed for two hearths in 1672; his inventory of 2 April 1701 mentions only one smithy, but in it two lots of smithy gears were valued together at £9 0s 0d, suggesting that the one building held two hearths. Robert Wainwright also had in his barn 1800 scythes worth £144 0s 0d together with debts and bonds owing to him worth £110 0s 0d.

The three cutlers in the 1672 list are not so

Tooles and Goods in the Three Shops

The tooles at the Woodsetts Smithy*	05li	02s	0d
The tooles in the smithies at home	04li	00s	0d
Four hundred of syths	25li	00s	0d
One Dosen of short syths	00li	10s	0d

*Extract from the inventory of Thos. Wainwright 16th October 1680 (LRO 1680-10-22). *Woodsetts is known now as Woodseats.*

well off as the scythe smiths. Two cutlers, William and Joseph Barton, were each taxed for one smithy hearth. In common with other names on the hearth tax list, Barton in various forms can be traced in parish registers over several generations back to the 1570s; many baptism entries give the father's occupation as nailer, scythe striker or cutler, although in the Barton family there were just as many husbandmen, tanners, shoemakers and carpenters. Joseph Barton died in 1683. His inventory records one smithy in which were a vice, a glasier, a cool trough, a saw, some iron and steel, hafts, tips and blades to the value of £1 17s 0d.

Joseph Jackson is described as a cutler, but no indication of this trade was given in his probate documents when he died in 1709. He would probably have been in his 40s in 1672 and had by the time of his death handed his business over to his eldest son, Richard. Joseph's wife, Troth, died in 1698 and the wording of his will hints at a situation which may or may not have resolved itself after his death. He bequeathed £10 0s 0d to his son Benjamin and another £10 0s 0d to Benjamin's son, Joseph, *"provided both return from beyond the seas in seven year's time"*.

Tools of the trade

Metalworkers of whatever occupation working on their own account and using their own or leased premises obviously needed tools, the tools of their trade. These tools, being part of the assets of a craftsman or woman, may be listed and valued in the inventory taken of the deceased's goods. When this is the case, the description of such tools can be valuable not just in identifying the tools themselves, but also in discovering whether the tools and the value put upon them have changed over the period under study and if so, how. However, for many reasons, in some inventories, no detailed list was made, the deceased craftsman's smithy tools or smithy gear being merely given an overall, undetailed value. In such cases other possessions seem few and of little value. In other inventories, bellows, stithy and tools were valued, plus an amount owing to the deceased for goods already supplied. It is as if the craftsman had ceased to work, still had assets in his gear and in the goods for which he was awaiting payment, but no longer needed to keep a stock of raw materials, such as iron, steel or the *coales* to which reference is sometimes made. A third category of documents appear to show that death occurred in the middle of a fully productive working life. Such inventories provide detailed descriptions of tools, stocks of raw materials and made goods, but it has to be said that the inconsistencies referred to earlier regarding the recording by the appraisers of the deceased person's possessions, whether to do with the household, the farm or the occupation followed, extended also to working tools. The reasons for the three categories found are based only on what appears to be the case from the detail given. Without firmer evidence any conclusions must be mere conjecture.

Table 4a shows five inventories over the whole period in which there are no details of any of the tools, merely a total overall value, recorded as *"smithie tools belonging to the trade"* or *"three smithies and tools"* or possibly just as "*Smythe ware*".

The condition of these smithy tools at the time of the deceased's death perhaps influenced the value placed upon them. One common feature of these five inventories is that

Date	Name	Occupation	Smithy tools value	Sum total
1547	R. Blythe	Smith/yeoman	£0 13s 4d	£13 7s 6d
1562	J. Blythe	Smith/yeoman	£1 0s 0d	£21 17s 8d
1683	R. Bingham	Scythe smith	£5 0s 6d	£51 8s 0d
1727	S. Biggin	Scythe smith	£2 2s 0d	£38 15s 6d
1750	E. Biggin	Scythe smith	£18 0s 0d *	£67 19s 6d

*3 smithies

Table 4a: Inventories showing undetailed smithy tools and value

Date	Name	Occupation	Smithy tools	With other	Sum total
1538	J. Alen	Smith/Yeoman	£1 0s 0d	Iron £3 0s 0d	£44 9s 1d
1572	R. Urton/Steven	Scythesmith	£7 0s 0d	Made goods £122 12s 0d	£152 7s 4d
1691	J. Gillot	Scythesmith	£8 0s 0d *	Tools wood £1 0s 0d + £4 0s 0d scythes	£593 16s 4d
1691	R. Gillot	Scythesmith	£8 0s 0d *	Tempering tools 8s 0d + scythes £16 0s 0d	£407 18s 6d
1719	S. Gillot	Smth/widow	£3 0s 0d	Made scythes £10 0s 0d	£36 9s 6d

* 2 smithies

Table 4b: Inventories showing smithy tools and other smithy goods value

none of the deceased men had any other items of craftsman's equipment, raw materials or made goods credited to them. They had perhaps ceased to work due to age or illness. Another feature is that the value of their farming goods occupied a high proportion of the sum total, so it would appear that, although the head of the family may have been unable to work, at least the small farm continued to provide a living.

It is possible using the detail in the five inventories in Table 4a and the five inventories in Table 4b listing working tools with other smithy items, to see how the value placed on smithy tools varied between different inventories, even if it is not possible to answer the question as to why there are such variations in value.

In all there were 35 inventories giving details of the metal workers' tools. In 24 of those the basic essential equipment of stithy (an anvil, the two words are synonymous) and bellows are either valued separately or along with one other small item. Even so, although the value of a stithy or a pair of bellows can be seen, there seems no discernible method in the valuation. The two stithies in the inventory of Robert Parker in 1535 are valued at £1 0s 0d each, whilst in 1557 Richard Malin's single stithy is given a value of £2 0s 0d. Later on in 1615 and 1622 a stithy is worth £1 10s 0d, compared with a value of £1 13s 4d for an old stithy in 1602 and 6s 8d for two old ones in 1623.

The same variations in value can be detected when looking at bellows. One pair is valued at £1 3s 4d in 1622, two pairs at £6 0s 0d in 1620 and 5s 0d for one pair of bellows and a cool trough in 1709.

Stithy and bellows are often valued together. In 1593 John Stevens' two stithies and two pairs of bellows were listed at £2 13s 4d; Robert Millward was a nailer whose stithy and bellows were valued at £3 0s 0d in 1623; and the two pairs of bellows and stithies belonging to Mary Atkin in 1724 were valued at £4 0s 0d; in the comprehensive detailing of Hugh Goddard's goods in 1695, the appraisers listed a pair of tempering bellows, one pair of bellows and a stithy at £2 0s 0d, two stithies and a pair of bellows at £3 10s 0d and one stithy and one pair of bellows at £2 10s 0d. The stithy in the Goddard inventory is called an anvil.

	li	s	d
In the upper smithye			
One paire of Bellowes one Anvill	2	0	0
A certaine parcell of Hammer and Tongs with other materialls	1	4	0
Cowltrow and Grindeing stone	0	9	6
Three dozen of old sithes and an od p(ar)cell of old iron	0	19	6
In the nether smithye			
One Anvill and one paire of Bellowes	2	10	0
Two dozen of ruff sithes Tempering Bellows	4	2	0
Two dozen of waster sithes	0	8	0
Cowltrow and Grindeing stone	0	6	6
Att Heeley			
Two Anvills and one paire of Bellowes	3	10	0
A p(ar)cell of Hammers and tongs	0	6	0
Three dozen of ruffe sithes at the wheele	1	16	0
In the Sithe stock in Debts and Sithes remaineing one hundred and fifty pounds	150	0	0

Extract from inventory of Hugh Goddard of Cliffield, scythe smith, 27th June 1695 (LRO 1695-10-02). Total value: £276 18s 0d.

The inventories of the cutlers in Norton during the period studied do not display much detail of their tools, although certain items of equipment, such as a vice and a glasier are common to most of them.

Two cutlers, Richard Bate, who died in April 1666, at the possible age of 68 years (Norton parish register records the baptism of a Richard Bate on 12 April 1598) and his son William Bate, buried on 6 September 1668, make interesting comparisons. Richard's only items of craft equipment were a vice and a foot glasier, valued at 12s 0d, but the sum total of his inventory was £151 14s 2d. This included £108 2s 0d in money owing to him, a bond worth £105 12s 0d and £2 10s 0d in desperate debts. When William died just over two years later the sum total of his goods was only £44 12s 0d. His craft items, a vice, a pair of bellows, hammers and tools belonging to the cutlery trade, were valued at £2 10s 0d. His father had bequeathed to him £60 0s 0d in money with a similar sum for him when land at Bixley near Norwich was recovered to the family, but there is no sign in William's inventory or will of this bequest. (Richard's total inventory value is more like that of his son when the credited £108 2s 0d is deducted from the total, making it £43 2s 2d)

One cutler was an exception, his tools being listed and valued in great detail. Robert Wildsmith made his will on 16 October 1615, two days before his burial. His inventory was taken on 24 October. Three out of the four appraisers of his inventory were cutlers; the value they put on his cutler's equipment was £6 7s 0d out of a sum total value of £41 8s 3d. This total should have been augmented by the £19 2s 6d owing to him by eleven men, one of whom, Robert Barnsley, owed £11 0s 0d and another, James Cominge of London, owed £1 1s 0d. There is no information as to whether these debts were ever paid or if the debt was for knives already supplied by Robert Wildsmith to each of these men as customers or agents. Even if they were paid in full, the fact that Robert Wildsmith himself was in debt to seventeen people for a total of £54 17s 8d meant that his estate when he died was worth a net total of only £5 13s 1d. The names on the list of those owing him money are locally familiar and the amounts vary from the £22 0s 0d owed to Thomas Ibbotson to 3s 6d owed to Dorothy Rodes; again there is no information as to what was concerned in the debt. The widow, Rosamond Wildsmith, was the execu-

	things in the smithie	li	s	d
Item	one paire of bellowes and the tew Iron	0	viii	0
Item	one stythie or anvile	0	xxx	0
Item	two Iron vices	0	xiii	iiii
Item	seaven hammers	0	vi	0
Item	4 paire of tonnges	0	0	xvi
Item	2 Footings of steele	0	0	xx
Item	certeien peices or p(ar)cells of Iron	0	iii	iiii
Item	two cuttlers sawes	0	0	xvi
Item	foure dozen of knyves	0	viii	0
Item	Nyne dozen of knyve blads	0	vii	vi
Item	certeine rapes and files w(it)h other little toyles	0	ii	0
Item	one whetteninge stone w(i)th an axeltree and a pulley one glasser w(i)th an axeltree and roughe grindlestones one other Iron axeltree and a pulley	0	xx	0
Item	certaine Knyve heafts and a peice of Olyvant	0	iii	iiii
Item	certaine other knyve heafts and knyve blads mooded	0	iii	vi
Item	one hacke and one axe	0	0	xiiii
Item	fyve knyves w(it)h sheathes	0	0	xii
Item	certaine knyves sheaths	0	xiiii	0
Item	one Emmery plate	0	0	vi

Extract from inventory of Robert Wildsmith, Woodseats, cutler, 24th October 1615 (LRO 1616-11-26). Total value: £41 8s 3d. From the context, it is presumed that "rapes" means "rasps".

trix, but there is no administrator's account to show whether any attempt was made to recover money owing. Doubtful though that outcome may be, it would seem that Robert Wildsmith died whilst in full working life, which may account for the number of items given in his inventory. The parish registers also show the baptism of a son, Richard, in January 1614 and another son, Robert, in February 1616, after the death of his father, but show no other events from which the fate of this family can be discovered.

Raw materials

There are references in 27 inventories to the iron and steel which were the raw materials used in the making of knives, scythes and sickles. More references could be hidden among the debts which some of the 61 metal workers owed to men who were probably their suppliers.

Two of the cutlers' inventories mention ivory (or oliphant, as it was then called) without giving a weight or a separate value to it. In 1615 Robert Wildsmith had one piece of ivory together with knife hafts worth 3s 4d whilst in 1625 Robert Cowley's appraisers valued his steel and ivory in total at £1 9s 0d.

As can be expected, the ways of recording iron and steel are many and various. Steel can be inventoried as burdens, hundred weights, packs or gads or, as in one case, footings, two footings of steel in Robert Wildsmith's inventory being worth 1s 8d. Sometimes steel is combined with iron in values ranging from 5s 0d in 1615, through 18s 6d in 1724 to £3 7s 8d in 1623 and £2 8s 0d in 1721. What amount was involved was not stated.

A burden of steel was a load of unspecified weight, usually taken to mean a cart load or what could be carried by a pack animal, although this does not seem enough to account for the difference in the value of the four burdens of steel in John Barnes' inventory in 1603 and the seventeen burdens in William Blythe's in 1632. Four burdens in 1603 were worth £30 7s 0d, i.e. £7 11s 9d per burden, whilst thirty or so years later, seventeen burdens were valued at £8 10s 0d, or 10s 0d per burden. One hundredweight of steel was valued at £1 0s 0d in James Atkin's inventory in 1683 and two packs of steel at £4 16s 0d in 1685.

A gad of steel is a wedge-shaped billet or ingot.[13] They were not valued highly; 135 gads in the 1640 inventory of Thomas Bower being worth 7s 4d; George Hobson had 120 gads in his inventory of 1672 valued at 8s 0d. In other words a gad of steel was worth ½d or ¾d. Robert Wainwright was a prosperous scythe smith whose inventory was taken on 2 April 1701. His craftsman's equipment was worth a total of £169 15s 0d, including £3 0s 0d for two hundred weight and four stone of what the appraisers called *"gade steel"*. Gads can refer to Flemish, Spanish or Swedish steel. What kind of steel Robert Wainwright had been using to make the 1800 scythes which were also valued in his inventory, is impossible to determine without firmer evidence. Certainly his is the only inventory in which such gad steel is referred to and valued by a precise weight, suggesting that it was steel of a special sort and of some value; Robert Wainwright's two hundredweight and four stone was worth £1 4s 0d per hundredweight.

Inventoried descriptions of iron appear as bar iron, smithy iron, dozens of ironstone, blooms of iron or parcels of old iron. Obviously some of the references are to iron in differing states, bar iron and smithy iron having been already processed for use in scythe making, whereas *"dozens of iron stone"* presumably refers to the ore bearing stone still in its raw state. William Blythe the elder's inventory was taken on 6 December 1620, his smithies then containing only raw materials. His appraisers valued eight blooms of iron at £6 0s 0d, (15s 0d each); 12 dozen ironstone at £6 0s 0d, (10s 0d per dozen); 21 pieces of iron by weight making up four dozen at £2 4s 0d, including a stithy coke; and five and a half dozen ironstone at £1 13s 4d. This latter ironstone was described as being at Coal Aston, just over the Norton parish boundary in the neighbouring parish of Dronfield and may possibly have been mined there. Scythe makers did use some local iron, although since its quality was not highly regarded, much of the iron they used was imported, as has been noted above.

Iron is referred to in five inventories. Its weight is given, enabling some comparisons to be made. James Batte had one ton of *"Amyas iron,"* (the meaning has not been found, but possibly refers to iron imported from Spain or Sweden) worth £2 13s 4d in April 1536. William Blythe in 1632 had two tons eleven hundred weight of iron worth £38 5s 0d. In 1666 one ton twelve hundredweight and six stone of iron was valued at £23 14s 6d and in 1683 one ton was worth £13 10s 0d. One hundredweight of iron was therefore worth between 13s 6d and 15s 0d, over the 50 year period from 1632–1683. The fifth inventory is that of John Barnes in 1642, in which eight burdens of steel and two hundredweight of iron were valued together at £6 0s 0d, a credible figure given the values of the iron and steel found in other inventories. Is it possible that the appraisers were not just consistent, but actually precise in their valuing of gads of steel, burdens of steel and hundred weights of iron? No evidence is ever given by the appraisers, who were nearly all of similar standing and occupation as the deceased, of any bills they may have seen on which they based their valuations of the accurate seeming weights of the iron and steel found on the deceased's property shortly after his death. Probate accounts might show such evidence as a will's administrators attempted to call in debts of credit or settle debits, but only one such account survives for Norton. Richard Bingham, scythesmith, died in August 1683, but his executrix's administration account (B/C/5/1684/11LRO) gives no detail regarding his two debts of £3 12s 0d and £7 0s 0d.

Nine inventories record and value what the appraisers called "coales" or "coles", the usual differences appearing here too. In only one inventory, that of John Barnes in 1642 (LRO

1647-05-25) is it clear that both sea coal and charcoal are present, although no precise amounts are given:

In the Smithy ....
Certaine seacole and Charcole   xv s

Was John Barnes using both charcoal and sea coal in his smithy hearth?[14] And was this a common practice? The low value suggests that there was not very much of either fuel, but other inventories record higher values and greater amounts. Sometimes the fuel is in loads, valued at amounts between 2s 0d and 3s 0d, although in Edward Hudson's inventory of 10 August 1622 *"coales by estimacon three loads"* are valued at only 4s 0d. At other times fuel is given in dozens, as in William Blythe's inventory of 1620 when *"coales by estimation 44 dozen"* in his smithies were valued at £26 8s 0d, (12s 0d per dozen). Only in the inventory of William Blythe on 17 February 1632 does there seem to be an attempt to distinguish between coal and charcoal; the appraisers recorded *"Certeine Coukes xs"* among miscellaneous items, *"Certeine Charcole iiiis"* in the bakehouse and *"six loades of Coles xviiis"* in William Kent's smithy.

Wood is mentioned in only a few inventories. In 1620 Thomas Hudson's twelve dozen of green timber was worth 9s 0d and in 1666 William Blythe had an unspecified amount of cordwood at his mill, valued at 13s 4d. Such wood was perhaps part of stocks of wood ready to be made into charcoal to fuel the smithy hearth.

Made goods

Out of the 61 sets of documents for the Norton metal workers, 27 contain references to the goods made by the deceased craftsmen. Four of these men were cutlers; one, William Bullock, although described in his will of 10 November 1666 as esquire, had numerous axes and hoes in his inventory and appears in the will and inventory list as the only axe smith. Thomas Hudson, whose inventory was taken on 19 October 1620 and whose precise metal working occupation is not clear, was credited with 13 sickles, valued at 13s 0d; presumably he was making them in his smithy. The only sickle smith was William Atkin in 1710 and he had no made goods in his inventory. The remaining 21 men were involved in scythe making, these implements in various quantities either being present on the deceased's premises when the appraisers made the inventory or appearing on the list of money owing to him.

William Bullock, lord of the manor of Norton, was buried there on 7 March 1667. The entry in the parish register gives his age as 50 years and refers to him as *"armiger"* i. e. esquire. He has the distinction of having the largest, most

Date	Name	Fuel	Value	Value per load
1603	John Barnes	Coales	£0 11s 0d	NV*
1620	Thos. Hudson	3 loads coles	£0 6s 0d	2s 0d
		7 loads coles	£0 14s 0d	2s 0d
1620	Wm. Blythe	44 dozen coales	£26 8s 0d	12s 0d
1622	Ed. Hudson	3 loads	£0 4s 0d	1s 4d
1632	Wm. Blythe	Coukes	£0 10s 0d	NV
		Charcole	£0 4s 0d	NV
		6 loads coles	£0 18s 0d	3s 0d
1640	John Barnes	Seacole & charcoal	£0 15s 0d	NV
1680	Thos. Wainwright	Coales for smithies	£1 10s 0d	NV
		Coales at wheel	£1 0s 0d	NV
1691	Rich. Gillot	Coles	£3 5s 0d	NV
1701	Robt. Wainwright	Coales	£1 0s 0d	NV

* NV = no value given in inventory.
Table 5: Inventories showing fuel used in smithies and its value.

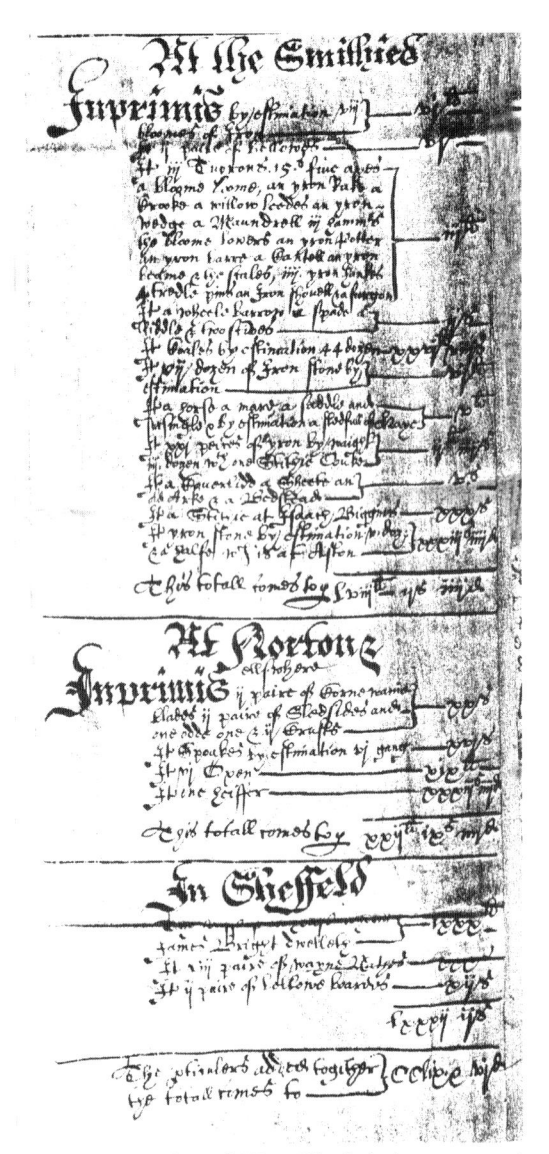

Fig. 4. A portion of Wm. Blythe's inventory, 6 Dec.1620 (LRO 1621-04-10).

complicated house and, at £895 17s 7d, the highest inventory value, of any of the men involved in metalworking. His craft goods, the axes and hoes referred to above, totalled £193 17s 6d in value and are listed thus in his inventory, their precise location at Little Norton not being given.

William Bullock was more likely to have been an entrepreneur employing other men than to have himself possessed or practised the skills necessary to make the axes and hoes which accounted for nearly £200 out of his total inventory value. More will be said later about another important Norton family which was concerned with the making of scythes over three generations, some members of which also appeared to be entrepreneurs.

The four cutlers in the inventory lists were not so prosperous. Richard Rose was a cutler whose goods when he died in 1556 were valued at £27 4s 4d. He owed William Dolphin 9s 4d for four gross of knife sheaths, but there is no sign of completed knives in his inventory. The only man described as a sheather in the Norton lists was John Anderton in 1630 and he had no made goods in his inventory.

Robert Wildsmith's inventory of 1615 has been quoted above and shows the total value of his stock of made goods as £1 17s 4d. The other two cutlers, Richard Cowley of 1625 and Joseph Barton of 1683 appear less productive; Cowley had £1 9s 0d of knives dressed and undressed valued with steel and ivory and Barton had 15s 0d worth of hafts, tips and blades valued with iron and steel.

By contrast, the picture provided by the detail in the scythe makers' inventories shows what appears to be a busy, active scene from the date of the first of the scythe smiths' documents to mention made goods, in 1567, until 1719 when Sarah Gillot's inventory suggests that, in her widowhood, she had continued in her husband's business. Scythes are mostly referred to in hundreds or dozens. A hundred scythes varied in value from £6 0s 0d in 1567, rising to £8 0s 0d in 1572, £8 13s 4d in 1642 and dropping slightly to £8 0s 0d again in 1701. The value given to dozens varied more. In 1622 it was 16s 0d per dozen; £1 1s 0d in 1640; and 15s 0d in 1716. An estimate for the value of 200, 4 dozen and 8 scythes in 1680 suggests 16s 0d per dozen, whilst another inventory in 1680 containing 1 dozen short scythes values these at 10s 0d per dozen. One dozen rough scythes, presumably unfinished, were worth 12s 0d in Hugh Goddard's inventory of 1695; other rough scythes mentioned were valued together with iron, steel or smithy gear; Robert

	Att Little Norton	£	s	d
Item	199 dozen of axes and 11 odd axes	100	00	0
Item	204 dozen of small howes	40	16	0
Item	122 dozen and a halfe of Larger howes	50	00	0
Item	Stithy bellowes and glaseinge wheele	01	13	0
Item	Iron att the smithy and William Bates and one Matax	01	08	6
Item	...............a debt of	13	00	0
Item	due to the dec(ease)d from Isaack Spooner w(ic)h is desperate	03	00	0

Extract from inventory of Wm. Bullock, 17th June 1667 (LRO 1667-10-17).

Gillot had 100 of these in 1628 and the £10 0s 0d credited to Sarah Gillot in 1719 included 20 dozen finished implements and 15 *"in the rough"*.

It was suggested above that someone such as lord of the manor William Bullock was more likely to have been employing the men who fashioned the axes and hoes valued in his inventory than to have been actively engaged himself in producing these goods. It was also suggested that another, locally much better known, family in Norton was in the same position and it is from the probate inventories relevant to this family, the Blythes,[15] particularly the two William Blythes later in the 17th century, that more can be learnt about the destinations of those bundles, hundreds, dozens and packs of scythes.

William Blythe died in February 1632, leaving his executors to pay his debts of £242 8s 6d. The names of twenty-one people are listed, including the Earl of Newcastle to whom he owed £9 0s 0d, and John Bullock to whom his debt was £45 15s 0d. The names seem to be mostly those of local people, but there is no clue as to what was comprised in the debt. The same applies to the eleven people who owed a total of £24 15s 1d to William Blythe. The total value of his inventory was £641 9s 8d and it is clear from the contents – his farming goods came to over £205 0s 0d – that he was a landowner as well as a 17th century industrialist. There was a corn mill at East Hall Meadow and a grinding wheel in Heeley on the River Sheaf; George Roper and William Kent were renting smithies from him, their names also appearing in the list of those to whom William Blythe owed money; 3s 0d was owed to Roper and Kent for hardening. It can be seen from Table 7 that William Blythe's workmen had been making four different kinds of scythe, described in his inventory as

Date	Name	Made goods	Value	Comment	Sum total
1556	Rich. Rose	None mentioned	£0 9s 4d	Owing for 4 gross knife sheaths (at 2s 4d)	£17 4s 4d
1615	Robt. Wildsmith	4 dz. knives	£0 8s 0d	2s 0d per dozen	£41 8s 3d
		9 dz. knife blades	£0 7s 6d	10d. per dozen	
		Knife hafts & oliphant	£0 3s 4d		
		Knife hafts & blades	£0 3s 6d		
		Knife sheaths	£0 14s 0d		
		5 knives with sheaths	£0 1s 0d	Total made goods £1 17s 4d	
1625	Rich. Cowley	knives dressed & undressed (with steel & oliphant)	£1 9s 0d		£62 2s 4d
1683	Jo. Bartin	(Iron, steel, hafts & tips of blades)	£0 15s 0d		£48 14s 8d

Table 6: Inventories showing values placed on made goods.

Date	Name	Scythes	Value	Comment	Sum total
1567	J. Bower	200	£12 0s 0d	£6 0s 0d per 100	£30 19s 3d
1572	R. Stevens*	1200	£96 0s 0d	£8 0s 0d per 100	£152 7s 4d
1593	J. Stevens			Scythes & weigh beam	£137 6s 0d
1603	J. Barnes			Scythes at R. Barnes' wheel	£132 14s 8d
1603	T. Came	2 dozen old	£0 18s 0d	9s 0d per dozen	£19 6s 4d
1622	E. Hudson	21 dozen	£16 16s 0d	16s 0d per dozen	£69 12s 0d
1623	G. Urton/Steven			£80 0s 0d CR for scythes & steel	£93 17s 8d
1628	R. Gillot	100 rough		With iron & steel	£72 12s 0d
1632	W. Blythe	650 long	£65 0s 0d	£10 0s 0d per 100	
		450 2nd sort	£40 10s 0d	£9 0s 0d per 100	
		450 3rd sort	£36 0s 0d	£8 0s 0d per 100	
		350 Scottish	£24 10s 0d	£7 0s 0d per 100	
				Total value £166 0s 0d	£641 9s 8d
1634	H. Brownell	200 + 4dozen+ 8	£17 5s 4d	Approx. £6 13s 0d per 100	£112 3s 6d
1640	T. Bower	9 dozen	£9 9s 0d	£1 1s 0d per dozen	£33 3s 4d
1642	J. Barnes	600	£52 0s 0d	£8 13s 4d per 100	£140 13s 10d
1666	W. Blythe	6 pack Scottish	£42 0s 0d	£7 0s 0d per pack**	
		260	£17 10s 0d	£6 15s 0d per 100	
		236	£13 16s 0d	£5 16s 6d per 100	
		2 dozen	£1 4s 0d	In transit £74 10s 0d	£561 18s 10d
1680	T. Wainwright	400	£25 0s 0d	£6 5s 0d per 100	
		1 dozen short	£0 10s 0d		£196 7s 2d
1686	E. Brownell	800 (at wheel)	£56 0s 0d	£7 0s 0d per 100	£593 16s 4d
1691	J. Gillot	Rough	£4 0s 0d	CR for scythes £61 19s 0d	£593 16s 4d
1691	R. Gillot	Scythes	£18 10s 0d	250?	£407 18s 6d
1695	H. Goddard	1½ dz. old	£2 10s 0d		
		3 dz. old		No value	
		2 dz. rough		No value	
		2 dz. waster	£0 8s 0d		
		3 dz. rough	£1 16s 0d	12s 0d per dozen (At wheel)	
		In stock remaining	£150 0s 0d	Total value £154 14s 0d	£561 18s 10d
1701	R. Wainwright	1800	£144 0s 0d	£8 0s 0d per 100	£373 6s 6d
1716	G. Turner	Scythes at Loxley	£102 0s 0d		
		6 dozen	£4 10s 0d	15s 0d per dozen	
		At smithies	£2 5s 0d		
		Owed to him	£103 13s 0d	Total value £212 8s 0d	£861 6s 6d
1719	S. Gillot	20 dozen+15	£10 0s 0d	(15 in rough)	£36 9s 6d
1724	T. Goddard	70 rough		With smithy gear	£110 13s 4d

* *Richard Stevens also had 12 packs of sickles valued at £2 4s 4d per pack, giving a total for sickles of £26 12s 0d.*
** *The values suggest that one pack = 100, the Scottish scythes presumably being packed for protection during transport.*
CR = credit

Table 7: *Showing made goods in scythe smiths' inventories in values per 100 or per dozen according to the inventoried values.*

long scythes at £10 0s 0d per 100, scythes of the second sort at £9 0s 0d per 100, scythes of the third sort at £8 0s 0d per 100 and Scottish scythes at £7 0s 0d per 100. The distinction between the four types is not clear, apart from their inferred length and the difference in their value per 100.

The contents of the inventory of William Blythe's son and heir, another William, taken on 22 February 1666, provides information about the distribution of his products and about three of his suppliers. His inventory total was £561 18s 10d. Just like his son, he too owed a considerable amount at the time of his death. Twenty-five people were owed sums ranging from the £39 9s 0d and £36 0s 0d due to his relatives Richard and Ellen Blythe respectively, down to the 2*s* 6*d* owed to Robert Holland. Once more there is no detail as to what the debt to these people with local names was for, but three names do offer a clue. William Blythe owed £30 0*s* 0*d* to Lionel Copley[16] and £45 0*s* 0*d* to Mr. Cotton,[17] both men being local ironmasters; another debt of £8 0*s* 0*d* was due to John Ardron, whose family had a forge at Orgreave, near Rotherham. Such debts were presumably for supplies of the iron used in making the scythes produced in his smithies. (Another local iron master supplying iron to the Norton scythe makers, was Godfrey Froggatt[18] who was owed £39 4*s* 0*d* by John Barnes in 1643 – see below.)

The money owed to William Blythe in 1666 and the scythes listed as belonging to him in his inventory make the area of distribution clearer. Four groups of scythes in transit are valued and described in this extract from William Blythe's inventory, dated 22 February 1666.

The list of seventeen people in debt to William Blythe includes the names of five people who owed money, presumably for scythes already sold in the named areas or in transit and awaiting further dispatch. William Belwood and Richard Bradley, both of York owed £3 10*s* 0*d* and £4 12*s* 0*d* respectively, Thomas Cowlin of Morpeth owed £3 6*s* 0*d*, John Butcher of Newcastle owed £3 0*s* 0*d*, and Mrs. Mary Gibson, also of Newcastle owed £1 0*s* 0*d* plus a bond in William Blythe's favour valued at £15 11*s* 0*d*. All of these people and the four quoted in the inventory extract, may well have been merchants, buying scythes to sell on to their customers, or they may have been innkeepers, acting as agents. A Mr. George Loop was taxed on eight hearths in Boroughbridge in 1672 and Thomas Horsfull (a variant of Horsefield) paid tax on nine hearths in the same year in Wakefield. Houses of such a size in market towns were often inns. The Smale family was well known in Beverley, three serving as mayors earlier in the 17th century.[19] None of the names can be related to carriers, an occupational grouping which is entirely absent from the Norton probate records.

The Blythes may have established a kind of trading monopoly on the Great North Road route and points in Yorkshire's East Riding. Certainly no other inventory reveals a connection with places to the north of Norton. However, another P.C.C. will, that of Thomas Biggen, scythesmith, dated 29 September 1605,[20] lists debts due to him from no fewer than 29 people, most of them in places north of the Norton/Sheffield area; the amount of each debt is given but in only four cases is the debt specified. Jervase Strelley of Beauchief in Norton parish owed Biggen £6 0*s* 0*d* to be set against the half-yearly rent for the wheel where Biggen worked; Robert Owtrem of Horsleygate, near Holmesfield in north Derbyshire, owed 33*s* 0*d* for an anvil, but was given the option of providing instead 22 stone of what was called Stanley iron; William Morris owed 2*s* 4*d* for a scythe; and Peter Foxe owed 6*s* 0*d* for grazing

At the house of Mr. Horsfeild in Wakefield	
4 packs of Scotch sythes and at the wheele 2 packs	£42 0*s* 0*d*
At Mr Loops house in Burrowbridge	
2 hundred and 5 dozen sythes	£17 10*s* 0*d*
At Mrs Smales house in Beaverlie	
2 hundred and 3 dozen holderness sythes	£13 16*s* 0*d*
At Mr Isles house in Yorke	
2 dozen of sythes	£1 4*s* 0*d*

Extract from inventory of Wm. Blythe 22nd February 1666. Total value of the scythes: £74 10s 0d (LRO 1666-02-28).

a heifer. Thomas Biggen's other creditors were in places such as Louth in Lincolnshire, Rotherham, Warmsworth, Harwood, Beverley, Cawood, Thorpe, Ryedale and Wensleydale, all in Yorkshire; Humbleton in Northumberland; Brough in Westmorland and Cockermouth in Cumberland (now both in Cumbria). Debts ranged between £10 0s 0d and 13s 6d; the total due to the testator was just over £153 0s 0d.

Four other places are mentioned in the Norton metal workers' inventories. Cutler Robert Wildsmith's inventory of 1615 lists £1 1s 0d due to him from James Cominge of London among ten other people whose names do not seem to be local. In 1604 Christopher Barton, nailer, was owed 14s 0d by William Bayliss of Retford. Scythe smith Thomas Bower in 1640 was owed 10s 0d by John Eastimer of Dunnam (Dunham) on the banks of the Trent in Nottinghamshire and £3 8s 10d by John Parker of Horncastle, in Lincolnshire. Samuel Steel of Darrington, near Pontefract in the West Riding of Yorkshire, is listed as owing £35 10s 0d to George Turner in the latter's inventory of 1716.

In the work done on the metal workers of the neighbouring parish of Eckington, published in *Tools and Trades*,[21] it was suggested from the places mentioned that their goods were sold in and around the area to the south and east of Eckington. The detail regarding any trade routes in the Norton records is sparse, apart from the information in the Blythe

Fig. 5. Now known as "Bishops' House" and in the care of Sheffield City Museums Service, this timber-framed house at Norton Lees was the home of the Blythe family. (Drawn by Edward Blore in 1823, Bishops' House as it appears in Sheffield City Museums Information Sheet 16.)

inventories and the Biggin will, but it can be argued that since two families had established such a grip on the outlets to the north, that other Norton scythe makers had developed contacts in markets to the south and east in Lincolnshire and beyond, in the same way as the Eckington sickle smiths had done.

The Scottish scythes are more problematical, but the customs accounts of Dumfries and Kirkcubright in 1589, 1590, 1592 and 1621 reveal that excise duty in those years was levied on imported agricultural tools, such as hooks, sickles and scythes coming across the Border from England.[22] Their place of origin is not stated in the accounts, so they may or may not have been made by the metal workers of north Derbyshire, but the fact that excise duty was levied is evidence of such a trade route. Dumfries and Kirkcubright were not the only places appearing in the customs accounts of burghs close to the English border and on trade routes across that border. Many dozens and packs of scythes, sickles, reaping hooks, wool shears and scissors appear in the customs books for Jedburgh, Kelso, Ayton and Duns near Berwick, and Alisonbank, the modern Gretna, between 1667 and 1686[23]; the latter place also recorded customs duty paid on five gross of penknives and on two gross three dozen knives in September and October 1672.[24] Merchants or agents and sometimes customers are named in the accounts for all these places, but never in such a way as to make it possible to identify the source of the imported goods.

Any discussion about the distinguishing features of a Scottish scythe seems to centre around perceived differences in the haft or sned, particularly the "Y" shaped one in common use in the north-east.[25] However, it is generally accepted that only the actual scythe blades were supplied by the craftsman.[26] The handle of the scythe was fixed to the implement by the purchaser, very possibly because of the fact that various styles had evolved in different parts of the country.[27] Therefore the variation in the value put on long, short, 1st, 2nd and 3rd sorts in the Blythe inventories must relate to the blade itself. (The same is possibly true of the Holderness scythes held at Mrs Smale's house in Beverley in 1666.) The answer to the question as to why the Scottish scythe was valued at £7 0s 0d per 100 both in 1632 and in 1666, compared to the lower value given to the other scythes in the 1666 inventory, must await the result of further research, but it is a tenable theory that the difference between the Scottish tool and the others lay in the blade itself.[28]

Debt and credit

Thirty-six of the metalworkers in this study had either debts to be paid or credits which their administrators would hope to collect. Twenty-one had no debts, but were owed money and three men owed money, but had no credits to be called in.

All the twenty-one who had creditors also had made goods in their inventories, but only in those inventories mentioned above is there any clue about the nature of the debt to the deceased. The smaller debts were possibly owed for small numbers of scythes or sickles, but it is difficult to know, for example, why Robert Barnsley owed £11 0s 0d to Robert Wildsmith, cutler, in 1615; what Henry Smith's debt of £59 3s 4d to Henry Brownell in 1634 was for; or why Thomas Spenser owed £11 0s 0d to James Atkin, sickle maker in 1683, the Spenser family being gentry ironmasters in the Sheffield area at this time.

There is more information either given or to be inferred about the debts owed by the metal workers, but even so, the great majority of their debts cannot be identified. An exception to this lack of informative detail, however, is in the inventory of Richard Rose, taken on 9 September, 1556. He owed a total of £2 10s 8d and was mentioned above as the cutler who owed 9s 4d to William Dolphin for four gross of knife sheaths; a man of this name appears in the neighbouring metal working area of Eckington between 1547 and 1558, but whether he was a sheather is not known. As to the other debts in the Norton metal workers' inventories, by using related local sources their nature can at least be guessed at.

Debts in some six inventories ranging in date from 1622 to 1716 can be attributed to purchases of iron and steel from local ironworks. Edward Hudson was a scythe smith whose inventory was taken on 10 August 1622. Among his goods were listed 21 dozen scythes valued at £16 16s 0d and debts owing to him from 13 people of £31 14s 0d, the sum total being £69 12s 0d. However, his own debts totalled £64 17s 6d, his appraisers ending the document by saying "*Summa de claro…£4 14s 6d*"; in other words once Edward Hudson's creditors were paid, there was little value left. Two of his debts were for steel:

To Will(ia)m Arthur for steele ………… £5 0s 0d
To Mr. Francis Moorewood for steele …… £8 14s 8d

Yet another debt for £14 0s 0d was to Sir Peter Frecheville and although this is not specified as being for iron or steel, it is likely that it concerns a purchase from the Frecheville family's furnace at nearby Staveley or perhaps the one at North Wingfield. Edward Hudson thus owed £27 14s 8d for the raw materials of which his scythes were made.

Scythe grinder Robert Gillot died in 1628 and in his inventory of 28 March are listed the rough scythes, iron, steel and grinding stones previously referred to. He owed £13 1s 4d to seven men and was in his turn owed £54 4s 0d. None of his debts is specified as being for iron or steel, but two names in particular are associated with local iron works. Robert Gillot owed Mr. Bullock £7 17s 0d; the Bullock family was prominent in north Derbyshire and certainly had ironworks in Norton and at nearby Beauchief about this time.[29] William Blythe and James More, two other names involved in the metalworking industry, were owed money by Robert Gillot; a single debt to William Blythe was for £3 12s 0d and that to James More and William Blythe £5 10s 0d. As was done for Edward Hudson, the appraisers of Robert Gillot's inventory neatly laid out the total sum of his goods and chattels as £59 10s 8d, separate from his credits of £13 1s 4d, making a total of £62 12s 0d and then list his debts of £54 4s 0d, making a net total of £8 8s 0d.

William Blythe's inventory, taken in February 1632, has already been mentioned. The sum total of his goods was £641 9s 8d, out of which £24 15s 1d was owing to him. Two sums of £3 4s 0d each owing by John Barnes and Roland Gillot were part of this, which may have been for the rent of their smithies. His debts amounted to £242 8s 6d and include £45 15s 0d to John Bullock, probably the same person identified in Robert Gillot's list of debts above. William Blythe may have been buying iron from this local ironworks too. Other debts, £60 3s 6d in all, were owed to the More family, Stephen, George and Henry's executors, but no proof that these debts were for iron or steel has been found; the name of More or Moore features in several of the metal workers' listed debts.

In May 1640 Thomas Bower's appraisers again neatly set out his few goods and chattels totalling £27 10s 6d, added to that total the £5 12s 0d of desperate debts he was owed and then listed the £36 1s 6d in money he owed to ten people. One of these debts, £2 7s 6d, was to Roger Hellifield. A man of this surname was involved later in the century in steel making in the district of Kimberworth, north of Sheffield, but whether the two were related is not known, nor is it certain that Thomas Bower's debt was for steel. What does seem without doubt is that Thomas Bower's executors were faced with a negative balance of £2 18s 2d even if all the desperate debts could be collected.

John Barnes had a comfortably furnished house and was well supplied with smithy gear, made goods and raw materials when his inventory was taken on 11 March 1643, his iron and steel being valued at £6 0s 0d. The sum total came to £140 13s 10d. He was owed £44 8s 0d by fifteen people, making a grand total of £185 11s 10d. He himself owed £60 8s 0d:

Godfrey Froggat was the servant of the Frecheville family at their iron works in Staveley. A William Warter was Master of the Cutlers' Company of Sheffield in 1645 and

Robert Brelsforth was possibly the same man who became Master Cutler in 1648. The Shemeld family were both tanners and cutlers in Sheffield.[30]

Debts outward to:	
Mr. Godfrey Frogatt for iron.	£39 4s 0d
Will(ia)m Warter	£9 12s 0d
Robert Brelsforth	£5 12s 0d
Will(ia)m Sheemeld	£6 0s 0d
Sum(ma) total.	£60 8s 0d

As we have seen, William Blyth's inventory of February 1666, totalling £561 18s 10d contains several debts to be paid for iron and steel, including a small debt to Robert Brelsforth, whilst the debts owing to him have already been referred to in the section dealing with the distribution of made goods. One name not previously found is that of Tooker, the man of that name to whom William Blythe owed £7 14s 0d belonging to a well known steel making Rotherham family; Thomas Tooker became Master Cutler in 1685.[31] The amount owed for iron and steel totals £92 6s 0d out of a total indebtedness of £204 15s 4d. Three other creditors in the list to whom William Blythe owed small amounts of money were Robert and John Holland and William Downes. The Holland family were London carriers in Chesterfield[32] and some members of the Downes family were also carriers, although no firm evidence has been found to link the names in William Blythe's list of debts with either of them. The last inventory to contain information about debts owed for raw materials is that of George Turner, taken on 3 April 1716. This man has already been mentioned as being more of an entrepreneur than a working scythe smith. The sum total of his inventoried goods was £447 12s 10d; £404 13s 6d was owing to him, which included £103 13s 0d for scythes made, the total sum thus amounting to £852 6s 4d. However, George Turner owed twelve people a total of £840 15s 0d; in his will dated 20 February 1716 he left instructions to his trustees and administrators to sell property in Hooton Pagnell in Yorkshire, in Sheffield and in Norton, to pay his debts and settle the legacies described in his will, excepting a leasehold house he had in Sheffield, which was bequeathed to his daughter, Ellen. The debts include £30 0s 0d for his funeral expenses, £130 0s 0d owed to Mr. Battie, the Sheffield attorney, £20 0s 0d to the doctors and apothecary and £8 15s 0d for rent due to Mr. Gregg and Mr. Nevile; his other debts amounting to £215 18s 6d are to eight named persons. Some of them belong to families well known as landowners in the Sheffield area; the Mr. Bright, to whom George Turner owed £200 0s 0d, was probably a member of the family which owned large acreages of woodland and also leased coal mines from the Duke of Norfolk: Mr. Burton may be William Burton, to whom George Turner owed £100 0s 0d – Burton was associated with wheel, forge and slitting mill sites on the Sheffield rivers, including the Loxley, the same river referred to in George Turner's inventory[33]. Turner may have bought his iron from Burton, although there is no firm evidence for this, nor is there any to show what the £12 0s 0d to Mr. Bamforth was for. George Bamforth II was the owner of Mousehole Forge on the Rivelin river just above its confluence with the Loxley as well as owning grinding wheels and Wisewood forge and rolling mill on that same river, so George Turner's debt could have been for rent.[34]

A dual occupation

Although the metal workers in the two north Derbyshire parishes of Eckington, the subject of previous research, and Norton, the parish under examination here, each had established their own spheres of specialisation, in neither place was the making of sickles and scythes the sole means of livelihood for them. In Eckington 30% of the metal workers' inventories studied showed evidence of dual occupation, based on the number of cattle, sheep and horses and the crops listed and evaluated in their probate inventories. In neighbouring Norton the figure could have been as high as 45%. 58 of the Norton metalworkers' inventories list farm goods. Some are of very low value, consisting only of a few implements. Others have few animals and little in the way of crops. Such men, involved in metal working of whatever kind, seem to have had so little in the way of farm goods that it is questionable whether they had a dual occupation. Other men, with numerous livestock and with several acres or day's work of growing crops, were farming in such a way as to be able to use that as a safety net at times of the year when demand for their craftsman's products was low or fluctuating. This situation is characteristic of a dual occupation. The value put on their livestock, crops and husbandry gear could amount to more than 50%, sometimes as much as 70%, of the total inventory value. In seventeen of the 60 metal workers' documents the term "yeoman" is used to describe the deceased; the appraisers of the goods would possibly designate him scythe smith, or cutler or another kind of craftsman, but when making his will, a man might say he was a yeoman, this term suggesting an inherited holding of perhaps between 30 and 60 acres, enough to allow a man to grow crops and breed livestock not just to provide for his family's needs, but also sufficient to bring in a small profit.

John Allen the elder, who died in September 1538, was such a yeoman. The total value of his inventory was £44 9s 1d, the farm goods being worth £25 11s 10d. He had wheat, barley, rye, oats and hay in his barn, together with oatmeal and malted barley, totalling £8 10s 8d; his livestock was valued at £16 6s 0d altogether and comprised 8 kye, a cow, 3 heifers and a bullock, 6 oxen, 19 sheep, a horse and a mare, 9 swine, 4 pigs and some poultry. As well as those items he also had £3 0s 0d of iron and £1 0s 0d of smithy gear. James Bate, whose inventory was taken on 20 April 1536, was another such yeoman metalworker. His inventory totalled £24 1s 5d, of which £14 0s 10d was derived from his farm goods. It being April, his crops were few, 13s 4d being the value given to four day's work of oats. However, his livestock value was £12 18s 2d for a cow, 4 kye, 2 heifers, a bullock, 70 sheep, a horse and a mare and some pigs. His craftsman's items were valued at £2 13s 4d for one ton of Amyas iron. John Bower was a scythe smith, who made his will on 22 March 1567. His inventory total was £30 19s 3d of which his farming items and husbandry gear came to £13 2s 0d. A cow and calf, 3 kine, 2 heifers, 15 sheep, ewes and lambs, a mare and foal and a pig totalled £10 16s 0d, whilst strikes and quarters of wheat, oats, barley and malt, with 6s 8d of sown hard corn came to £2 2s 0. His craftsman's items included £12 0s 0d, the value given to his 200 made scythes.

The seventeen yeomen craftsmen include several families over the whole period. One notable example is that of the Urton/Stevens. Their five inventories range from 1572 to 1630 and all relate to Lightwood, one of the outlying farmsteads of Norton. The earliest, Richard Urton/Stevens, is described as a scythe smith, the four later family members as yeomen. Richard Urton/Stevens had £122 0s 0d of made scythes and sickles in his inventory of 12 August 1572 out of a total value of £152 7s 4d; he also mentions in his will of that year that he has bought a tenancy in Norton from Jerome Blythe of London. Richard Urton/Stevens' brother, Henry, died in 1591 and John Urton/Stevens the elder in 1593. Both men had smithy gear, but also had farming items worth 53% and 59% respectively of their total inventory value, comprising for each of them, five or six cows, heifers, stirks, oxen, a bull, several calves and horses. Their crops too were valuable; oats, wheat, rye and barley were listed either in a barn or sown in the fields. For John Urton/Stevens 34 acres of oats, hardcorn and peas were valued in several different named fields. George Urton/Stevens died in May 1623. No crops were mentioned or valued and only one bay gelding with saddle, bridle and girths is listed. He did, however, have £80 0s 0d as a credit for his stock of steel and scythes. As suggested earlier, he may have been ill and unable to work. He was the son of John Urton/Stevens junior, who died seven years later with an inventory value of £219 13s 0d out of which the farming goods came to £161 1s 0d.

The Gillots were another family of yeomen

scythe smiths, whose wills and inventories give details not just of land which they held and were bequeathing to their heirs, but also of a most profitable involvement in scythe making. Robert Gillot of Lees in Norton died in 1628 and has already been mentioned above in the section on grinding stones; he also had 100 rough scythes and iron and steel to the value of £12 0s 0d. His farming items totalled £21 18s 8d out of a sum total of £72 12s 0d. Both John Gillot of Woodseats in Norton and Richard Gillot of Bolehill had high value inventories of £593 16s 4d and £407 18s 6d respectively. John Gillot's crops, livestock and husbandry gear totalled £79 17s 0d and his smithy and wheel tools came to £14 10s 0d. He was also owed £61 19s 0d for scythes already made, out of a total credit sum of £231 19s 0d. Richard Gillot died in the September of the same year. His farming goods totalled £60 19s 0d and the equipment and tools in his two smithies, iron house and at the wheel were valued at £53 4s 6d altogether. Not only that, he had £160 0s 0d of silver in a chest.

These men and others like them, who were not classed as yeomen, were obviously following a dual occupation. Their farming inventories list valuable crops and many animals, including horses and their sum totals are among the highest of the metal workers.

The Blythes of 1632 and 1666, with the earlier Blythes of 1546, 1562 and 1620, are familiar from previous discussions, as are William Bullock, gentleman axe smith of 1667, and George Turner, scythe smith of 1716. To them might be added Robert Parker of Little Norton in 1535, John Parker, esquire, in 1616 and George More, gentleman, of Greenhill in 1623. Their wealth came from the fact that they were landowners, both of farmland and raw material sites, and owners of smithy and grinding wheel sites. Their inventories list made goods, but probably as employers of labour rather than as working craftsmen themselves. They certainly had valuable crops, livestock and husbandry gear and the detail in their inventories adds to the knowledge of agricultural practice, but, although they are of great importance in the overall metalworking scene, they do not fit into the category framework for the kind of dual occupation where a man worked on his farm and in his smithy in order to support his family.

The metal workers of Norton, 1533–1750, made up 20.4% out of the total number of occupations and categories found in the probate records; of these metal workers, the scythe smiths, at 47.5%, were by far the most numerous group, giving Norton its significant place in the industrial history of north Derbyshire and later in the 17th century, in that of Hallamshire, as the area six miles round Sheffield and over the Derbyshire border was called.

Important the scythe makers may have been, and they may have given Norton a distinguishing feature, but they were only one part of the whole. In the community too were yeomen, husbandmen, widows, gentry, many craftsmen and clergy. The story of these people, their houses and their possessions remains to be told.

References
1. K. M. Battye, "Sickle Makers and other Metal Workers in Eckington, 1534-1750", *Tools and Trades*, Vol. 12, September, 2000.
2. P. Riden, "The Population of Derbyshire in 1563", *Derbyshire Archaeological Journal (D.A.J.)*, Vol. 98 (1978), pp. 61-71.
3. D. G. Edwards, "Population of Derbyshire in the Reign of Charles II", *D.A.J.*, Vol. 102 (1982), pp. 106-117.
4. David Crossley, ed. "The Sheaf", *Water Power on the Sheffield Rivers*, Sheffield, 1989, p. 104; Norton parish registers (PR), Sheffield City Archives (S.C.A.)
5. All dates quoted as from parish registers and dates of baptisms, marriages and burials are taken from Norton PR in S.C.A.
6. Battye, *op. cit.*, p. 28.; K.M. Battye "Probate Records as a Source for the Study of Metal Working in Eckington, 1534-1750", *D.A.J.* Vol. 119 (1999), p. 297 *et passim*.
7. Crossley, *op. cit.*, p. 102.

8. D.G. Hey, *Packmen, Carriers and Packhorse Roads*, Ashbourne, 2001, p. 100; *Historic Hallamshire*, Ashbourne, 2002, p. 112.
9. Hey, *Packmen*, p.
10. Prob/11/109 PRO, *supra*
11. (Derbyshire) *Scarsdale Hearth Tax 1672*, (PRO E179/94/394).
12. Crossley, *op.cit.*, p. 98.
13. Webster, *Dictionary of the English Language*, Gad ... a wedge-shaped billet of iron or steel. 1913. Rosemary Milward, *A Glossary of Household, Farming and Trade Terms from Probate Inventories:* gad (of Spanish iron) ... a bar of iron, Derbyshire Record Society (D.R.S.), 1982. Steel was also imported from Sweden.
14. The term "sea coal" originated from the surface coal outcrops on the coast of northeast England, being picked up on the beach without the need for underground coal mining. The mediæval term eventually became the generally used one for all mineral coal. (Information from the editor.)
15. The Blythe family is associated with Bishops' House, Norton Lees, now part of Sheffield. The timber framed house, although much altered, still stands and is now in the care of Sheffield City Museums.
16. Lionel Copley was a prominent figure in the Yorkshire iron industry, with interests in ironstone mines, charcoal woods, furnaces and forges. P. Riden, "George Sitwell's Letter Book, 1662-1666", *D.R.S.* Vol. X, 1985, p. 43; D.G. Hey, *The Fiery Blades of Hallamshire*, pp. 70-1, 174, Leicester, 1991.
17. William Cotton was an ironmaster, the tenant of forges at Wortley, Kirkstall and Colnbridge in Yorkshire West Riding and of a furnace at Barnby. Riden, *op.cit.* p. 43.
18. Godfrey Froggatt of The Hagge, Staveley, Derbyshire, was a servant of John Frecheville, landlord of Staveley ironworks. Riden, *op.cit.* p. 44.
19. Information supplied by D. G. Hey.
20. Prob/11/107 PRO
21. Battye, *Tools and Trades, op. cit.*
22. A. Murray, "Customs Accounts of Dumfries and Kirkcubright, 1560-1660", *Dumfries and Galloway Natural History and Antiquarian Society*, Vol. xlii, 1965, pp.125-129; K.M. Battye, "Aspects of an English Export Trade", *Review of Scottish Culture no. 15*, 2002-3, pp. 120-122.
23. Customs Books, National Archives of Scotland, Edinburgh; Jedburgh, E72/13/1: 1 Jan. – 11 Oct. 1667; Kelso, E72/14/4, E72/14/5: 1 Nov. 1680-Aug. 1682; Ayton and Duns, E72/4/1: 25 Nov. 1680 – 1 Aug.1681; Alisonbank, E72/2/1: 1 Dec. 1665 – 31 Aug. 1666, E72/2/3: 1 Aug. 1672 – 1 Nov. 1672.
24. E72/2/3 *op. cit.*
25. A. Fenton, *Scottish Country Life*, East Linton, 1999, p. 61.
26. Information from Prof. D. G. Hey and B. Read.
27. Fenton, *op. cit.*, pp. 60-66.
28. Catalogues from three edge-tool manufacturing firms, one in north Derbyshire and two in Sheffield, in the late 19th and early 20th centuries show Scottish pattern scythes as being apparently lighter in weight and narrower in blade than other patterns made. Firms referred to: Thomas Staniforth & Co., Hackenthorpe, Sheffield. C.T. Skelton & Co., Sheffield; John Harrison & Sons, Dronfield, near Sheffield. (Information from K. Hawley, The Ken Hawley Collection Trust, University of Sheffield.)29. Crossley, *op. cit.*, pp. 102-3.
30. C. Binfield, and D. G. Hey, eds. *Mesters to Masters, a History of the Company of Cutlers in Hallamshire,*. Oxford, 1997, pp. 21, 317.
31. Hey, *op. cit.*, p. 185; Binfield and Hey, *op. cit.*, pp. 14, 317.
32. P. Riden, *History of Chesterfield*, Vol. II, Part 1, Chesterfield, 1984, p. 179.
33. Crossley, *op. cit.* pp. 9, 18, 43.
34. Crossley, *op. cit.* p. 43.

Appendix 1: Abbreviations

Place names:

BLH	Bolehill
BLHL	Bolehill
CLFD	Cliffield
CLFDYT	Cliffieldyate
DBLN	Derbyshire Lane
GLKWHL	Garlickwheel
GRN	Greenhill
HMS	Hemsworth
JDN	Jordanthorpe
LGHT	Lightwood
LS	Lees
LSHL	Lees Hall
LTNTN	Little Norton
MGR	Maugerhay
NLS	Norton Lees
NTN	Norton
SCKH	Sickhouse
TRTHS	Trouthouse
WDST	Woodseats
WDSTDL	Woodseats*d*ale
WNTN	West Norton

Occupations, etc.

CT	Cutler
G	Gentleman
NLR	Nailer
SCK, sck.	Sicklesmith
SCY, scy.	Scythesmith
SCYGR	Scythegrinder
SHTHR	Sheather
SMTH, smth.	Smith
WD	Widow
Y	Yeoman

Other

gds.	Goods
N.W.	No will
PR	Parish Registers
ST	Sum total
Tls.	Tools
Tmp.tls.	Tempering tools

Appendix 2: Glossary

Amyas iron	meaning not found, but possibly Spanish or Swedish iron.
Axxletrees	axletree; a beam or bar connecting two wheels on the ends of which the wheels revolve.
Cowltrow	a cool trough of water into which the smith plunged the hot iron.
Emmery	abrasive polishing material.
Glasier, glasser	glazing wheel used by cutlers for polishing knife blades.
Glasier, foot	a glazing wheel operated by foot, possibly using a treadle.
Grindlestone	Grindstone
Hard corn	wheat and rye mixed.
Harthstaff	tool for *d*rawing burnt material from hearth.
Howes	presumed to be hoes.
Kine, key, kye	cows, usually milking cows.
Landiron	large type of cob iron supporting burning wood.
Li, li	from the Latin = £
Mooded	an early part of the welding process before the linear forming of the string.
Olivant, olyvant	ivory.
Rapes	rasps.
Sallet	light armoured helmet, curving outwards behind.
Sheather	a maker of knife sheaths.
Sned	haft.
Stedde, stiddie	stithy, anvil.
Stirk	a young bullock, between 1 and 2 years old.
Tew iron	pipe from bellows to base of smith's hearth fire.
Thissell	thixel or adze.
trindles	wheels, usually in pairs.
Vice, vise	clamp used by cutlers
Waster scythe	an imperfect scythe
Whettening, whitin	a whetstone used for smoothing or sharpening blades.

Appendix 3: Norton Metalworkers.

A complete alphabetical and chronological list of the Norton probate material is held in the Sheffield City Archives.

LRO Pro/Ad	Inv Date	Will Date	Stnd.srn.	Forename	Place	Occupation	S.T.
1536-04-25	1535-00-00	1535-04-08	Parker	Robert	LTNTN	SMTH/Y	£16 4s 10d
1536-04-25	1536-04-20	1536-03-18	Bate	James	NTN	SMTH/Y	£24 1s 5d
1538-10-02	1538-09-13	1537-10-03	Allen, eldr.	John	HMS	SMTH/Y	£44 9s 1d
1545-05-12	1547-02-19	1546-05-07	Blythe	Robert	WDST	SMTH/Y	£13 7s 6d
1556-09-17	1556-09-09	1556-08-15	Rose	Richard	GRN	CT	£27 4s 4d
1557-04-27	1557-04-08	1555-06-10	Malin	Richard	WNTN	SMTH/Y	£55 8s 6d
1566-04-23	1562-00-00	1562-10-06	Blythe	John	LS	SMTH/Y	£21 17s 8d
1567-09-17	1567-00-00	1567-03-22	Bower	John	HMS	SCY	£30 19s 3d
1574-04-20	1572-08-12	1572-08-08	Urton	Richard	LGHT	SCY	£152 7s 4d
1591-09-20	1591-03-01	1591-09-22	Urton	Henry	LGHT	SMTH/Y	£124 1s 2d
1591-01-26	1591-09-00	N.W.	Thorpe	Chris.	WDST	SMTH	£13 4s 0d
1593-06-21	1593-01-12	1593-04-12	Urton	John, eldr.	LGHT	SCY/Y	£137 6s 0d
1604-03-31	1603-01-28	1602-06-30	Camm	Thomas	GRN	SCY/Y	£19 6s 4d
1604-03-31	1603-02-04	1603-01-20	Barnes	John	BLH	SCY	£132 14s 8d
1604-10-29	1604-06-30	1604-06-22	Barton	Chris.	WDSTDL	NLR	£78 6s 9d
1615-11-02	1615-10-20	1614-10-16	Holland	Robert	JDN	SCY	£74 3s 8d
1616-11-26	1615-10-24	1615-10-16	Wildsmith	Robert	WDST	CT	£41 8s 3d
1616-04-10	1616-01-04	1615-12-16	Parker	John	LSHL	SCY/ESQ	£386 17s 10d
1620-12-13	1620-10-19	1620-09-06	Hudson	Thomas	SCKH	SMTH/Y	£169 11s 4d
1621-04-10	1620-12-07	1620-09-08	Blythe	William	NLS	SMTH/Y	£259 0s 6d
1622-10-18	1622-08-10	1622-06-14	Hudson	Edward	SYK	SCY	£69 12s 0d
1623-05-26	1623-05-07	1623-00-00	Urton	George	LGHT	SCY/Y	£93 17s 8d
1623-04-30	1623-05-28	1623-01-03	More	George	GRN	SMTH/G	£253 15s 10d
1623-12-10	1623-09-29	N.W.	Millward	Robt. eldr.	NTN	NLR	£75 2s 8d
1625-06-01	1625-02-14	1625-01-04	Cowley	Richard	NLS	CT	£62 2s 4d
1628-09-10	1628-03-28	N.W.	Gillott	Robert	NLS	SCYGR	£72 12s 0d
1630-02-04	1630-01-02	N.W.	Anderton	John	WDSTS	SHTHR	£47 13s 4d
1630-12-07	1630-11-29	N.W.	Urton	John	LGHT	SMTH/Y	£219 13s 0d
1632-11-21	1632-02-17	1632-01-24	Blythe	William	NLS	SCY/Y	£641 9s 8d
1634-00-00	1634-00-00	1634-01-02	Brownell	George	MGR	SCY	NA
1634-08-23	1634-08-14	1634-01-23	Brownell	Henry	JDN	SCY	£112 3s 6d
1640-07-10	1640-05-15	N.W.	Bower	Thomas	NLS	SCY	£33 3s 4d
1647-05-25	1642-03-11	1640-10-18	Barnes	John	GLKWHL	SCYGR	£140 13s 10d
1666-02-28	1666-02-22	1666-02-28	Blythe	William	LS	SCY/G	£561 18s 10d
1666-09-18	1666-05-07	1666-04-04	Bate	Richard	GRN	CT	£151 4s 2d
1667-10-17	1667-06-17	1666-11-10	Bullock	William	NTN	AXSMTH	£895 17s 7d
1669-03-31	1668-09-02	1668-07-23	Bate	William	LTNTN	CT	£44 12s 6d
1672-10-17	1672-05-08	1672 admin	Hobson	George	TRTHS	SMTH	£30 13s 10d
1680-10-22	1680-10-16	1680-10-08	Wainwright	Thomas	CLFDYT	SCY	£196 7s 2d
1683-09-18	1683-06-01	1683-05-26	Warter	Thomas	CLFD	SCY	£35 2s 7d
1685-10-27	1683-09-05	1680-09-30	Barton	Joseph	WDSTDL	CT	£48 14s 8d
1683-09-18	1683-09-12	1683 Bond	Bingham	Richard	LGHT	SCY	£51 8s 0d
1684-03-26	1683-12-28	1684 Bond	Atkin	James	LGHT	SMTH	£54 3s 4d
1686-04-21	1686-03-20	1686-02-21	Brownell	Edward	CLFLD	SCY	£178 14s 4d
1691-10-14	1691-06-18	1691-05-13	Gillott	John	WDST	SCY/Y	£593 16s 4d
1691-10-24	1691-09-09	1691-08-04	Gillott	Richard	BLHL	SCY/Y	£407 18s 5d
1695-10-02	1695-06-27	1695 Bond	Goddard	Hugh	CLFLD	SCY	£276 18s 5d
1701-04-04	1701-04-02	1701-03-21	Wainwright	Robert	NLS	SCY	£373 6s 6d
1701-11-12	1701-10-23	N.W.	Parker	Joseph	NTN	SMTH	£4 17s 01d
1704-10-04	1702-00-00	1702-04-01	Goddard	William	CLFD	SMTH/Y	£25 17s 5d
1709-04-27	1709-04-20	1709-03-31	Jackson	Joseph	WDSTS	CT	£10 6s 2d
1709-07-20	1709-07-20	1709 admin	Thorpe	Robert	NTN	SMTH	£18 17s 10d
1710-11-14	1710-10-12	1710-08-03	Atkin	William	LGHT	SCK	£119 16s 0d
1712-09-30	1712-09-18	1712-08-05	Gillott	Joshua	BLHL	SCY	£100 7s 7d
1716-04-04	1716-04-02	1716-02-20	Turner	George	NLS	SCY	£861 6s 6d
1719-04-09	1719-00-00	1719-02-04	Gillot	Sarah	WDST	SCY/WD	£36 9s 6d
1722-04-04	1721-00-00	1721-09-12	Wainwright	John	NLS	SCY	£31 12s 0d
1724-09-30	1724-04-02	N.W.	Goddard	Thomas	DBLN	SCY	£110 13s 4d
1724-09-30	1724-09-23	1724-08-12	Atkin	Mary	SYK	SMTH/WD	£21 0s 1d
1728-04-10	1727-10-27	1728 admin	Biggin	Samuel	LTNTN	SCY	£38 15s 6d
1750-05-17	1750-04-17	1750 admin	Biggin	Ezra	LTNTN	SCY	£67 19s 6d

The author
Kathleen M. Battye worked as a part-time tutor with the University of Sheffield's Division of Adult Continuing Education for just short of 20 years, running classes researching probate wills and inventories, parish registers and census returns, and lecturing on the history of north Derbyshire. She retired in 2000 and returned to Scotland.

She has researched and published a history of the village where she lived as well as several other articles and has had the occasional paper published by the Derbyshire Record Society, using the research from her classes.

Fig. 1. A 17th century jointer plane dated 1682.

Folk craftsmanship in fruitwood: A seventeenth-century jointer plane dated 1682

Jonathan Green-Plumb

The theme of this short paper is an early woodworking plane. The following information is taken from the plane in question and from similar recorded examples in recognised literature. The intention is to discuss how such tools can be related to the time and place of making, how and why they may have been adapted and most importantly the possible reasons for their preservation.

It is possible to find thousands of tools from the 20th century and there are still relatively large numbers of tools extant from the 19th century. But go back another hundred years and the quantity of tools significantly decreases. There probably were not as many tools made then as with later periods due to a smaller population, thus fewer trade and craftspeople requiring them. The consequences of time and often neglect have resulted in relatively few tools surviving. In the terms of 18th century commerce, tools in this country were manufactured in large quantities, reflected in the thriving export trade, particularly to America. To date commercial planemaking in the Britain can be traced back to the end of the 17th century, when makers such as John Davenport were in business. Prior to this it seems likely that trade and craftspeople made their own tools with the assistance of blacksmiths for metal parts.

In the context of the above it is rare to find tools from the 17th century or earlier, especially in comparatively good condition, although many do survive in museums throughout the world, as discussed by Goodman[1] and Greber.[2]

One of the reasons why tools from this epoch have survived is because individuals and museums have collected them, even though such objects have now become redundant, in the sense that they are no longer functioning. Another reason is that many tools have been made in such a way as to be more than just utilitarian. The aesthetic qualities of objects seems to be a significant reason for conserving them.

The plane illustrated in Fig. 1. originates from the last quarter of the 17th century and apart from the overall size, which is perhaps the most unusual feature, it bears a date, owner's initials, religious symbols and chip carved decoration. The clear and distinctive date may well have been a deciding factor as to why this object has survived. Some time ago the iron and wedge were lost, making it functionless as a plane unless restored.

In 1682, somewhere in Europe, a tradesman was making this plane from a piece of fruitwood. (It seems to be pearwood though it may be cherry.) In that year Charles II had only three more years as a monarch before him and Christopher Wren had just been elected President of the Royal Society. Elsewhere, William Penn had arrived in Pennsylvania, where he was to found Philadelphia, and in Russia, Peter I and Ivan V became joint tsars.

Although at first glance this plane offers many idiosyncratic features, the maker would, perhaps like many others, have been working within a culture that collectively held beliefs about the nature of making objects. These may be considered constraints or simply accepted traditions. In a practical sense there is often a slight tension in items that display a desired balance between aesthetics and function as a starting point even before they are made. Most tools are made in such a way as to be dominated by their intended function. The more abstract, narrative and self-expressive elements can sometimes be overshadowed but are no less fundamental.

The 1682 date on this plane, as stated, is a significant reason for its preservation (Fig. 2). Early tools are very difficult to date accurately. Many tools have changed little over the past

Fig. 2. Detail of the date.

centuries in either their form and function. The style of the numbers, especially the eccentric number "1", together with other features, suggest that this plane was made in the Tyrol region of central Europe. Planes with similar stylistic features and dated 1678, 1755 and 1796, illustrated in Greber, are all attributed to that region. Another plane, this time a tongue plane with fence dated 1794, also has the same unusual "I" in its date.[3] A plane dated 1643 although not attributed to the same area also clearly fits in with those discussed and illustrated by Greber (Fig. 3).[4,5] It displays not only a similar style of dating to the 1682 plane in question but also has a similar escapement and chip carved decoration. Other objects from the late 17th and early 18th centuries display similar dates, as with the French bread cutting board illustrated (Fig. 4).[6]

Apart from the date, heart shaped escapement and chip carving, etc. this jointing plane has other features synonymous with decorated tools from the Tyrol area. Like many other early European planes it has a tapering stock and, particularly, "peg" handles. Overall the plane is 44⅜ in. long and at its widest point (just behind the mouth) is 4⅞ in. wide tapering to 4⅛ in. at the heel by means of a beaded chamfer. At the deepest point, though the centre of the escapement, the stock is 3 in. deep. This again tapers down to 2¾ in. at both heel and toe. The width of the mouth would suggest that a 3 in. iron was used.

Fig. 4. Detail of an 18th century French oak bread cutting board.

Initially the plane appears to be a cooper's jointer plane, taken out of service and subsequently used as a more generalised jointer. However, on closer inspection the "steps" cut out of each of the ends are crudely done, with the one on the toe having two holes roughly bored into it. The lack of sophistication in the workmanship and discrepancy in the patination confirms that these were done as alterations rather than original features. Judging by the accumulation of general dust and effects of oxidation, it would appear that these alterations were done a considerable time ago. The fact that coopers' jointers are used stationary with the sole uppermost and often with the heel on the ground would account for this plane now having its two rear handles missing.

The richness of patination on the two remaining handles would indicate that they are original or very early replacements. A more decorative jointing plane with two mouths and dated 1796 in the Tyrolean Folk Museum[7] has handles of not dissimilar form (Fig. 5).

With its large surface area these types of planes offer plenty of scope for applied deco-

Fig. 3 Plane dated 1643 after Museum Studies 2.

Fig. 5. An 18th century jointer plane in the Tiroler Volkskuntsmusuem, Innsbruck, after W.L. Goodman's History of Woodworking Tools.

ration. The date is accompanied by the maker's/owner's initials "LP", three crosses and two clusters of chip carving (each end of the top surface). The date, initials and crosses are homogenous, united by being formed through the application of repeated punch marks. The crosses are situated in front of and behind the escapement with the third directly in front of the foremost handle. The use of such religious symbols is quite typical of continental tools from the period and many authors have made extensive references to this form of personalising tools (Fig. 6).[8,9,10]

Another feature of the plane are the grooves that have been applied to each of the sides. Both are approximately ⅝ in. above the sole and are ½ in. wide. My initial thoughts were that these grooves were made using a plane, perhaps a moulding plane with a convex sole. However, the grooves are not straight, for when the plane is viewed over its span there is a pleasing inconsistency to them. Also they do not have the smooth "planed" finish. They have a serrated texture which implies the use of a toothed cutting iron. One possible explanation is that these features were formed using a scratch stock with a serrated or toothed iron. Greber illustrates several planes with this groove or channeling.[11] Clearly they were done to facilitate a firmer grip for the plane user. On this jointing plane though, they seem pointless, as an average hand cannot span the breadth of the stock. This begs the questions, were they applied purely as a traditional / customary feature, regardless of function?

Several authors have stated that planes were often made using poorer quality timber, as their prime stock would have been saved for customer's products.[12,13] The timber used

Fig. 6. A close-up view showing the crosses in front of and behind the escapement and the rose head nail reinforcement.

to form this plane could certainly fall within this assumption. Part of the side of the plane and particularly along the side of the escapement initially appears to be missing. However, on closer examination, the area concerned is covered with bark (Fig. 7). A flawed piece of timber, or was the maker fortunate to find a piece of fruitwood of this size at all? I would veer on the side of the latter. The flaw in the stock has required a compromise with the wedge retention lug on that side reinforced with an early rose-headed nail. The signs of considerable usage would suggest that this flaw made little impact on the plane's function.

The patination of the whole plane is subtle and delicate, almost contrary to its mass and form, and is undisturbed. The combination of years of use, oxidization and the accumulation of dust and dirt have left a rich surface colour. It was recently de-accessioned from a well-known American museum and thankfully it has avoided the fate of many tools on the open market, that of being over-enthusiastically cleaned and polished.

Woodworking and other tools are now firmly embedded in the culture of collecting objects from the past. A great deal of emphasis is place on condition and quality, and items in mint condition with original packaging are especially highlighted. In this context does it make sense to obtain, preserve and research a plane that has been altered, damaged, has the iron, wedge and handles missing, has been repaired and was originally made from flawed material?

If that object is of genuine historical interest and can be accurately attributed to a period and place, I believe there is no question to answer.

References

1. W.L. Goodman. *The History of Woodworking Tools.* London, 1964
2. Josef. M. Greber. *Die Geschichte des Hobels.* Hanover, 1987
3. Greber, illustrations 100, 101, 151, 124
4. Barbara Wriston. *Museum Studies 2.* Chicago, 1967
5. *Ibid.*
6. Robert Young. *Folk Art.* London, 1999
7. Greber, illustration 124
8. C. Proudfoot and P. Walker. *Woodworking Tools.* Oxford, 1984
9. G. Heine. "Man and his Tools – Customs, Beliefs and Practices", *Tools and Trades.* Journal of the Tool and Trades History Society. Vol. 5. 1988
10. G. Reinthaler. *Hammered Symbols.* Battle, 2003
11. Greber, illustrations 94, 128, 137
12. Arnold & Walker *Catalogue No. 6.* London, 1978
13. Rees, J. & M and others. *The Tool Chest of Benjamin Seaton.* London, 1994.

The author

Jonathan Green-Plumb obtained a BA in Fine Art Sculpture at Wimbledon and then an MA at Winchester School of Art. He currently teaches Design and Technology in a Norfolk comprehensive school. He is a keen amateur woodworker and has been studying and collecting early European woodworking tools for approximately 15 years. He is particularly interested in decorated or decoratively made and dated items.

Fig. 7. A view of the side of the plane near the escapement showing the poor quality of the timber, the bark covering this area.

Book Reviews

Antique Tools and Instruments
Luigi Nessi and others
Milan, 2004

Hard cover, 363 pp., numerous illustrations.
ISBN 88-7439-124-2
£48 in UK, available from Roy Arnold, 77 High St, Needham Market IP6 8AN .

Elton W. Hall

Perhaps some TATHS members have been aware of a quiet, enthusiastic, patient collector who speaks Italian and has been collecting the finest of tools and scientific instruments in Europe for the past thirty years. The collection formed by Luigi Nessi of Lugano, Switzerland, is surely one of the finest of its kind in the world. This book, comprising a part of the Nessi collection, is among the most important books yet to be written on the subject of tools. It deals with aspects of the subject at once very broad and very limited. The types of objects considered include scientific instruments, the tools of tradesmen, household implements, kitchen utensils and kits of implements for personal grooming. Yet within that extensive range, only the finest examples in terms of design, materials, and workmanship are included. They come principally from Europe and date from the Renaissance through the 19th century.

The important contribution this book makes to the literature on the history of tools and instruments is achieved in three ways. The first is that it is based on a great collection. Trained as an architect and urban planner, Nessi developed an interest in the tools used to produce the buildings upon which he worked. That led to a broader interest in tools of all sorts, which he began to collect. Possession of the objects nurtured an intense desire to know more about them, to document his collection, and to understand the cultural context in which they were produced and used. In the 1970s he abandoned his architectural and planning practice to devote himself to collecting both objects and information about them. The results of thirty years of vigorous pursuit of these materials are stupendous and provide the principal matter for the book.

The second element is that to supplement his own extensive knowledge, Nessi has invited five other scholars with considerable expertise in specific segments of the collection to contribute essays. In his introduction, Nessi first describes his goals, the parameters of his collecting utilitarian objects, their cultural context, and the rise in the production of objects possessing remarkable quality. He goes on to provide an overview of the kinds of documentation he has collected or studied to support his collection: contemporary images in many media, manuscripts, and printed sources. Peter Plaßmeyer, Director of the Mathematisch-Physikalischer Salon at the Dresden State Art Collections, contributed the essay, "Scientific Instruments as Tools: an Outline of Their Development from the Sixteenth to the Eighteenth Century." This and subsequent essays provide the opportunity for illustrations of some of the greatest examples of objects from public collections in Europe. Following each essay is a section of illustrations of relevant material from the Nessi collection, accompanied by captions providing the basic catalogue information about them. Marie-Veronique Clin, Curator of the Paris Musee de l'Histoire de la Médecine, wrote on "Surgical Instruments as Art Objects." Alessandro Cesati, architect and specialist antique dealer in Milan, treated "Civilization and Its Tools." This section deals with the tools of mechanics and tradesmen, their origins, development, and the impulse of many makers to strive for excellence and artistic merit in their production. Richard Wattenmaker, Director of the Archives of American Art of the Smithsonian Institution, has taken one material for his essay: "Objects of Contemplation and Pleasure: Wrought-Iron European Cooking and Fireplace Utensils of the Early Modern Era." Claudine Cartier, Conservateur en chef du Patrimoine-Inspection Generale des Musées in Paris, provided the last chapter: "From Personal Grooming to Individual Leisure: Objects intended for Private Use." These objects include tools for ladies and gentlemen to perform work suited to their stations: sewing, needlework, tape-making, knitting, writing, and snuff-taking. There are also travel boxes for ladies and gentlemen, containing equipment for personal grooming and dining. These are obviously intended for the upper classes, for they are generally in fine materials and richly decorated. In all these sections, the illustrations from the Nessi collection are carefully chosen and plentiful.

The third way that this book achieves its quality is that it is a handsomely produced book, well designed and printed. Its publication in Italian and French as well as English will greatly enhance its worldwide usefulness. Most importantly, the photography and colour printing has been executed to a very high standard. Thus the book itself was made a suitable vehicle for the splendid objects it describes.

Early Planemakers of London: Recent Discoveries in the Tallow Chandlers and the Joiners Companies
Don & Anne Wing
Marion, Mass. 2005

Softcover, 86pp, colour illustrations throughout, 3 foldout maps & charts
ISBN 0-9767459-0-9
£18.95 in UK, available from Roy Arnold, 77 High St, Needham Market IP6 8AN

In the first edition of *British Planemakers from 1700* Bill Goodman related how his discovery of the origins of English planemaking had followed "largely [as] a matter of luck" from the discovery of a plane marked ?ENNION and the chance acquisition of a "rather curious ogee moulding plane stamped ROBERT WOODING" which had prompted him to search the records of the Joiners' Company. His discovery of the Granford-Wooding-Jennion master-and-apprentice sequence, the business it supported, and the network of planemakers it trained has remained not only the core but effectively the sum of our knowledge of the nascent trade in the late seventeenth and early eighteenth centuries for almost forty years. While the researches of Jane and Mark Rees and others have greatly increased our understanding of the trade in the later eighteenth century and beyond, and thoughtful papers by Matthew Carter and Phillip West have shed some light on the dawn years of the trade, this immensely attractive period around 1700 has remained mysterious.

By what they modestly represent as a similar stroke of luck to Goodman's, Don and Anne Wing bought an early English moulding plane on eBay in 2003 which, when it arrived, turned out to be marked IOHN GILGREST. Searching apprentice names on the internet, they found, in the Tallow Chandlers Company records, the master-apprentice sequence John Davenport – John Gilgrest – George Carpenter which has led them to the further, extensive researches in Livery Company records, Court records, Rate Books, Poll tax records, Insurance Company records and Marriage Licence Allegations, the results of which they set out in this beautifully-illustrated book.

We have had a foretaste of the quality of the Wings' research and scholarship in their 1998 publication *The Case for Francis Purdew*, which demonstrated that all but one of the existing planes attributed to Thomas Granford were in fact made by a man known previously only as an apprentice of Robert Hemings, and which established the existence of a second planemaking master-apprentice sequence and business outside the City of London. This new book builds on the basis of that study, continuing its approach and presentation. The contribution it makes, however, is on a wholly different scale, representing an increase in knowledge as great, in the view of this reader, as that originally made by Goodman.

The Wings have brought the total number of planemakers known to have been working in London before 1750 to thirty-seven, and provide apprenticeship and in many cases freedom dates for them. This doubles the number previously identified, and dates many of those known or suspected to have been planemakers through the survival of marked planes. Examples include John Anderson, Richard Mealing, John Gilgrest and Joseph Hayes. They have also identified, later in the century, Sam Cox, John Bush and James Wignall. They show that there were two William Loveages and two Samuel Holbecks, and that John Davenport is not who we thought he was. Of the thirty-seven, sixteen were in the Joiners Company, sixteen in the Tallow Chandlers, and five in the Blacksmiths, Distillers and Haberdashers companies. They provide a splendid fold-out wallchart setting out the master-apprentice relations and chronology of the thirty-two joiners and tallow chandlers and some ninety apprentices bound to them or their masters whose subsequent occupations are presently unknown.

They also show, on reproduced contemporary maps, how the workshops producing wooden tools and planes were grouped in seven discrete areas, two within (the Joiners businesses) and five outside (the Tallow Chandlers and others) the walls of the City of London. Their researches indicate that the structure of the wooden tool and planemaking trade was very much more complex (and perhaps fluid) than has been generally thought. The romantic traditional notion of the rural master craftsman at his bench, with his apprentice and his cat, at the back of the shop in which his wife and daughter sell what he makes could only exceptionally have provided a model in early eighteenth century London. Then, as now, small manufacturing businesses were as likely to rely on wholesale and contract work as on retail, and to switch between them as need and opportunity dictated, adjusting resources appropriately by taking on and laying off journeymen and, in extremity, turning over apprentices. One of the Wings' most significant discoveries is that the master-planemaker William Reynolds, who began the Tallow Chandlers line which included Davenport, Heydon and Elsmore, appears to have been brought in from the country, already trained, by the ironmonger Richard Ingram, to whom he was hurriedly apprenticed when the ruse (which would have challenged the restrictive practices of the organized London trade) was detected. The evidence strongly suggests that the workshops outside the City worked principally to supply the ironmongers and thus the export and wholesale trade; indeed the Wings argue persuasively that they may also have supplied the Wooding firm, which was as much a factoring as a manufacturing business. That, if it is the case, would explain why so few planes survive marked by the Tallow Chandler makers (though not why so few survive marked by Granford, of whose earlier output, marked with his initials, they have found and illustrated an example).

The three chapters setting out these new discoveries form the core of the book. The two introductory chapters which support them contain much that is new (the section on ironmongers and plane iron makers promises much to come), and the two which succeed them, *Problematic Planemakers* and *Features of Early Planes*, as much again. The discussion of style in this latter chapter benefits particularly from the well-chosen and beautifully-reproduced illustrations which are a feature of the book.

Bill Goodman knew, when he searched the Joiners records, that the company's members were joiners only "in the sense that they had joined the Joiners' Company... they could be of almost any trade... Gingerbread maker, chimney doctor, Pawnbroker..." and that, by the same token, there would be joiners (and planemakers) in other Livery Companies. But he still looked only in the logical places – the Carpenters', Coopers', Shipwrights' and Turners' companies. How delighted he would have been to have seen the fruits of the Wings' discoveries, and how much he would have admired their scholarship and industry (even if he would not have entertained all their speculations).

Everyone interested in woodworking planes, in eighteenth century tools, their manufacture and the men who made them should have this book.